W9-AUM-549

Location of the area covered by this guide

High Sierra
Hiking Guide #6

Devils Postpile

by Ron Felzer

with the editors of
WILDERNESS PRESS
Thomas Winnett
editor-in-chief

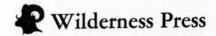 **Wilderness Press**

BERKELEY

Acknowledgments

This guide could never have been written without the help of many people. For the first edition, I appreciatively reacknowledge the advice and assistance of Stan Bunce, Dick Rea, Genny Schumacher Smith, George Hilton and Lorri Pehoushek.

For the second edition, I am eternally grateful to Danica Radulevich, John Derby, Arnie Albrecht, Bud Bowden and Gary Morgan of the U.S. Forest Service; fellow mountain men Dennis Danielson, Dan Williams and Al Fleischman; Mercedes Foster of the University of California; and to Tom Winnett (for both editions), the best and most long-suffering trail-guide editor ever.

—Ron Felzer
Berkeley, California
November, 1975

Second edition May 1976

Library of Congress Card Number 75-44822

ISBN: 911824-50-2

Manufactured in the United States

Introduction

The HIGH SIERRA HIKING GUIDES are the first *complete* guides to the famous High Sierra. Each guide covers *at least* one entire 15-minute U.S.G.S. topographic quadrangle, which is an area about 14 miles east-west by 17 miles north-south. The inside front cover shows the location of the area covered by this guide.

There is a great and increasing demand for literature about America's favorite wilderness, John Muir's "Range of Light." To meet this demand, Wilderness Press has undertaken this guide series. The purpose of each book in the series is three-fold: first, to provide a reliable basis for planning a trip; second, to serve as a field guide while you are on the trail; and third, to stimulate you to further field investigation and background reading. In each guide, there are a minimum of 100 described miles of trails, and the descriptions are supplemented with maps and other logistical and background information. HIGH SIERRA HIKING GUIDES are based on firsthand observation. There is absolutely no substitute for walking the trails, so we walked all the trails.

In planning this series, we chose the 15-minute quadrangle as the unit because—though every way of dividing the Sierra is arbitrary—the quadrangle map is the chosen aid of almost every wilderness traveler. Inside the back cover of this book is a map of the quadrangle showing the described trails. With this map, you can always get where you want to go, with a minimum of detours or wasted effort.

One other thing the wilderness traveler will need: a permit from the Forest Service (for federally designated wilderness areas) or from the National Park Service (for national-park backcountry). The Park Service permits have been in use for years; the Forest Service permits were instituted in 1971. You may obtain a permit at a Park Service or Forest Service ranger station or office by indicating where you are going and when you will be there. The Forest Service requires a permit for a day hike as well as a backpack. The two services will reciprocally honor each other's permits for trips that cross a boundary between the two types of wilderness. The Forest Service permits are also available by mail. For westside entry into the Minarets Wilderness, write Sierra National Forest, North Fork, CA 93643. For eastside entry into the Minarets Wilderness, write Inyo National Forest, Box 148, Mammoth Lakes CA 93546. For eastside entry into the John Muir Wilderness, write Inyo National Forest, 873 N. Main St., Bishop CA 93514.

The Ritter Range from the Muir Trail

Table of Contents

The Country . . . . page 1

The History 3

The Geology 5

The Flora 7

The Fauna 14

The Climate 19

Backpackers 21

The Trails 23

Trail Descriptions

    Day Hikes 25

    Backpack Trails 35

    Lateral Trails 78

Bibliography 85

Index 86

The Country

GAZING WEST FROM Minaret Summit, near the eastern edge of the quadrangle, the first-time visitor to Mammoth Lakes and the Devils Postpile country is stunned with awe at the grand vista below.

The jagged, knife-edged Minarets, products of volcanic activity nearly 150 million years ago, dominate the skyline. Mt. Ritter and Banner Peak, the highest points in the quadrangle (at 13,157 and 12,945 feet, respectively) stand to their right. This is great country to climb in.

Fifteen hundred feet below the viewer is the glacially scraped and rounded canyon of the Middle Fork of the San Joaquin River, which rises north of Banner Peak at Thousand Island Lake and flows across the quadrangle from north to south. Way off in the southwest, the impassable canyons of the lower Middle Fork and the lower North Fork merge on their way to slake the thirst of the Central Valley. There's plenty of water here.

More than a dozen year-round streams drain the backcountry. Over 50 trout lakes in glaciated basins dot the mountainsides. Twenty glaciers and hundreds of snowfields keep them flowing and cold. This is great country for fishing.

Inyo National Forest and Devils Postpile National Monument maintain 15 automobile campgrounds in the quadrangle. There are more than 150 miles of backcountry trails with innumerable campsites. Hiking and backpacking possibilities abound.

Behind the viewer is Mammoth Mountain, an ancient volcano. Red cinder cones are just out of sight to the south. To the north and east are explosion craters and an earthquake

Left: Rainbow Falls

fissure. Then there is Devils Postpile itself, down near the
Middle Fork of the San Joaquin. In this quadrangle the
geologist has a field day.

A variety of plant communities—from yellow-pine forest
to alpine fell-fields to sagebrush scrub—beckon the botanist.

The first-time viewer perusing this vast and varied environment has many possibilities here, whether he is a car-camper,
sightseer, photographer, angler, naturalist, hiker or mountain
climber. He may become one of the many who return again
and again. Though the land visible from Minaret Summit may
lose some of its novelty, it will remain "not a place to make
time, but to spend it."

The Ritter Range from Minaret Summit

The History

INDIANS DISCOVERED THE Sierra long before mountain man Jedediah Smith in 1827 led the first crossing of the range by Europeans. Several parties under Joseph Walker went through Owens Valley and passed by Mono Lake between 1834 and 1846, but for several years after, whites had little impact on either the Yokut Indians to the west of *Devils Postpile* quadrangle or the Paiutes in the Great Basin country to the east.

Yokuts and Paiutes had been trading over Mono Pass for hundreds of years before a cavalry detachment—in pursuit of Yosemite Indian Chief Teneiya—first crossed the Sierra in this region in 1852, going down Bloody Canyon, which lies just north of our quad. These soldiers soon returned to the west side, bringing back little more than some observations on gold-bearing quartz veins and obsidian domes east of the Sierra.

The demise of the native American way of life in this part of the Sierra was begun by the Gold Rush in the Mother Lode to the west and by mining activities in the Comstock Lode to the north. In the Mammoth Lakes region, this destruction of a gentle people came in the late 1870s. The killing of game and the destruction of natural forage by cattle were among the processes that forever disrupted the lives of the native inhabitants east of the crest. Most of the Paiutes who weren't killed off by white ranchers and miners went to work for them.

Probably the most significant early event in the development of human influence in this quadrangle was the incorporation of the Mammoth Mining Company in 1878. "Bonanzas" that didn't work out nevertheless led to a flurry of mining activity in the Mammoth Lakes area from 1877 to 1880. In

1878 the 54-mile Mammoth Trail, from Fresno Flats to Mammoth City via Reds Meadow and Mammoth Pass, became for stockmen, ranchers and prospectors a direct route across the Sierra to Mammoth Lakes. The droughts of 1863-64, '71 and '77 drove stockmen to the mountains for summer grazing. Sheepherding continued as far east as Summit Meadow until 1963. Mining at Mammoth City was pretty much a bust by 1880, but prospecting and spasms of activity in the late 1890s and again in the 1920s continued to open up the country.

In 1907 President Theodore Roosevelt proclaimed the formation of Inyo National Forest, consisting mostly of acreage in Owens Valley. Today half of our quadrangle lies in Inyo National Forest and half in Sierra National Forest. This land is administered by the government largely for recreation and watershed purposes. Devils Postpile National Monument, established in 1911, is the only other large ownership in the quad. So the main economic activities in this area have progressed from spates of mining and grazing to recreation, with some timber harvesting as well.

These changes have not come about painlessly, and such problems as overdevelopment around Mammoth Lakes and the status of the corridor between the Minarets Wilderness and the John Muir Wilderness—which leaves open the possibility of a road across the quadrangle—will have to be dealt with in the future.

The Geology

LANDFORMS RESULTING from vulcanism and glaciation dominate the landscape of *Devils Postpile* quadrangle. Pumice flats, red cinder cones and ancient lava flows attest to the past upheavals of this land. U-shaped canyons, hanging valleys, and scraped and polished rock faces show the grinding force of the most recent Ice Age glaciers.

Expanses of a porous, lightweight volcanic rock called pumice cover much of the eastern portion of the quadrangle. Pumice is a grayish, glassy rock full of holes created by gas bubbles when the rock formed. This material was deposited after the last Ice Age, less than 10,000 years ago, blown from vents that lie on a line from Mammoth Mountain to Mono Lake. These vents were formed when superheated gases and lava blew into the air at weak spots in the earth's crust.

Devils Postpile, from which this quadrangle takes its name, is itself a product of vulcanism. Approximately 630,000 years ago dark, molten lava of a type called andesite poured through Mammoth Pass and flowed down the canyon of the Middle Fork of the San Joaquin River. Here the liquid rock cooled, solidified, contracted and cracked to form columns having from three to seven sides. Later, glaciers scraped the tops of these vertical columns and left a beautiful, tilelike surface of glacial polish that can still be seen today.

As much as any other geologic process, glaciation has determined what the traveler in *Devils Postpile* quadrangle experiences. During the last approximately three million years, the Sierra experienced at least three major glacial periods. These were times when winter snowfall greatly exceeded summer

snowmelt, ice fields formed, and rivers of ice began to flow
down from the high country. These glaciers carved out glacial
basins, called cirques, surrounded on three sides by narrow
ridges, called arêtes, which the ice never overtopped. Glaciers
in large canyons, like that of the Middle Fork of the San
Joaquin, cut deeper than the tributary glaciers, leaving the
tributary valleys "hanging," with waterfalls coming down
from them—such as Shadow Creek.

As these rivers of ice advanced, they scraped, gouged and
plucked vast amounts of material from the underlying rock,
and pushed and carried this material to lower elevations. When
the glaciers melted back, they left ridges of piled rock called
moraines along the sides of canyons and across them.

Glacial polish, which is especially evident along the Shadow
Creek Trail and between Reds Meadow and Fish Valley,
evinces the grinding force of the ice. Further testimony to the
glaciers' power are the *roches moutonees* seen along the North
and Middle forks of the San Joaquin. A *roche moutonee* is a
large hump of rock with a steep downstream face, where the
glacier plucked material away, and a gently sloping upstream
side, planed by the advancing ice.

The very recent glacial erosion is one important reason that
most canyon walls are so devoid of vegetation compared to
canyon floors. The ice scoured the canyon walls and deposited
the material on the canyon floors, where it developed into soil
hospitable to plant growth.

Geological events, modified by the effects of climate, determine not only what rocks we walk on during the day, but also
to a large degree what plant cover we sleep under at night, and
even whether there's wood for a campfire.

The Flora

THIS CHAPTER EMPHASIZES that part of the flora we call trees. Not only are trees the most evident members of the plant kingdom in *Devils Postpile* quadrangle, but they exert the greatest influence on environmental conditions that determine what other plants and what animals are to be found. Trees affect the incoming solar energy and the outgoing reflected and reradiated energy, and hence affect the temperature. They modify atmospheric humidity. They modify the wind; they change the very earth itself by their root actions, and by their litter of dead leaves, limbs and trunks which eventually return to the soil.

Lodgepole pine (*Pinus Murrayana*) is far and away the most abundant tree in the quadrangle. It is found from 7000 to 10,000 feet in elevation, and from canyon bottoms to windswept summits. Lodgepole is easily distinguished from all other conifers in the region by its 2-inch-long needles grouped in bundles of two; its thin, scaly, light-colored bark; and its short, prickly cones, which may remain closed and on the tree for several years. This latter feature ties right in with the ecology of the species.

Lodgepole pine belongs to an amorphous group of plants called "pioneer" species because they are among the first to enter and establish themselves in an area that has been disturbed. Sometimes lodgepole cones remain closed until the heat of a forest fire opens them to release the seeds. The winged seeds are easily carried by the wind onto burned areas, landslides, avalanche slopes and road cuts, where they quickly germinate and cover the ground with a dense growth of seedlings.

This pioneering character of lodgepole pine is tied in with the species' intolerance of shade. Seedlings do very poorly under the cover of larger trees—even parent lodgepoles—and regeneration is much better in openings than under the forest canopy. That is one reason why, in meadows throughout our quadrangle, lodgepole-pine forest is succeeding grasses. If seedlings can get started in the generally heavy turf of meadows, they grow fast, because of favorable light and moisture conditions. Fires, which kill both small and large lodgepoles, and sheep, which kill just about everything, have tended in the past to keep High Sierra meadows in what ecologists call a "sub-climax" condition, consisting of grasses and herbs. These non-woody plants withstand the onslaught of grazers better than trees because of their shorter life cycles. However, Smoky the Bear and restrictions on grazing in the mountains have led to the invasion of many meadows—Summit Meadow in particular—by lodgepole pine. Eventually the shade-tolerant but fire-intolerant firs may succeed even lodgepole pines in this ecological process. Firs replacing themselves would be the "climax" community here.

Another pine, found generally at somewhat lower elevations and on drier sites than lodgepole, is Jeffrey pine (*Pinus Jeffreyi*). It was named for its discoverer, John Jeffrey, an early Scots botanist who, when the Royal Society was slow in sending him his stipend, walked off into the Mojave Desert never to be heard from again. Jeffrey pine is similar to ponderosa, or yellow pine, a species found mostly lower down on the west slope of the Sierra and not at all in *Devils Postpile* quad east of the Sierra crest. Jeffrey is distinguished by its large, stiff cones (to 12″) and the heavily vanilla- or root-beer-scented bark of older specimens. Its 5-10″ needles are nearly always in groups of three, and they often appear from a distance to be clumped at branch ends. Jeffrey may be distinguished from lodgepole pine not only by its needles but also by its bark, which is dark and furrowed on young trees and reddish in large plates on older ones.

The ecology of Jeffreys contrasts with that of lodgepoles in that Jeffreys are more fire-resistant, due to thicker bark, and tend to form uneven-aged stands of trees of varying ages, compared to the more homogeneously aged groves of lodgepole. Its roots were used by early California natives in basketwork.

Jeffrey pine ranges from Oregon to Baja California, and in *Devils Postpile* quadrangle it is normally found between 6000 and 9000 feet. It is common on the trail to Cascade Valley.

Silver pine, or western white pine (*Pinus monticola*), is one of two 5-needle pines encountered in our quad. The other is whitebark pine. "Five-needle pines" are those whose needles are grouped in bundles ("fascicles") of five. Within this group are also sugar pine, limber pine, bristlecone pine and eastern white pine. Silver pine's flexible-scaled cones are 5-10″ long, and its bark is brownish and blocky.

Once the mainstay of the timber industry in Idaho, this species is being wiped out commercially in the northern part of its range by white-pine blister rust. This disease, which attacks all 5-needle pines, was brought into this country in the late 19th century on seedlings from Europe. Like many introduced parasites, blister rust had no natural enemies in the new habitat, and its new hosts had no immunity to it, so it spread fast and destructively. An interesting feature of this fungus' life cycle is that it lives on 5-needle pines for part of its life and

on members of the genus *Ribes*—gooseberries and currants—for
the other part. Both groups of plants have to be present for
the parasite to exist. In *Devils Postpile* quadrangle both hosts
are commonly found, but blister rust has not yet spread this
far south in the Sierra.

Silver pine does not occur in pure stands, but is scattered at
elevations from 8500 to 9500 feet, especially in the Mammoth
Lakes basin.

The other 5-needle pine commonly found in this quad is
whitebark pine (*Pinus albicaulis*). This is *the* timberline species
of the Sierra; it clings to windswept, rocky slopes up to 11,000
feet. Its whitish, flaky bark and its small, purplish cones—often
broken open by Clark nutcrackers to get the pine nuts—distinguish it from silver pine.

Whitebark pines generally look like trees according to the
definition which says a tree has a "single main stem un-
branched for several feet above the ground and a definite
crown," etc. But often they appear to be prostrate, ground-
hugging shrubs, due to high winds and deep, long-lasting
snows. These elements of whitebark pine's environment force
the tree into a horizontal growth form—known as *krummholz*—
rather than the upright habit it is genetically programmed for.
Any branches and buds which in some summers grow above
the others on a plant and stick above the snow level are sum-
marily killed the following winter by wind-blown particles of
ice and snow. The plants therefore grow away from the wind,
often along the ground, and often on the leeward side of a
boulder. On barren summits, high winds blow most winter
snow away before it melts into the ground. Hence, whitebark
pines on high ridges are living under essentially arid conditions,

and can be considered quite drought-resistant. Their ability
to survive without much water is especially evident along the
Deer Lakes Trail on Mammoth Crest.

Under crest-line conditions such as these, the tree grows
very slowly, and past use of this species for firewood in subalpine regions has greatly depleted the amount of wood
present. We recommend against the use of whitebark pine
for fires, and standing dead trees especially should be left as
they are because their esthetic qualities far outweigh their
thermal values.

Fir trees are members of the pine family but are easily distinguished from the pines, and usually from each other. There
are two firs in this part of the High Sierra.

California red fir (*Abies magnifica*) has flattened, four-sided
needles, which are *not* grouped into fascicles on the branches.
Another distinguishing characteristic of the species is its upright, barrel-shaped cones—up to 9″ long by 3″ in diameter—
which disintegrate on the tree in the fall and are not found
whole on the ground unless they have been cut by squirrels or
blown down by high winds. The true firs are the only conifers
in the Sierra that have upright cones. Red-fir bark is gray and
thin on young trees, but red and thick, with deep furrows, on
older specimens.

This species is not resistant to fire, especially when young,
and it is absent where frequent ground fires favor the more
resistant Jeffrey pine or the pioneering lodgepole pine. However, several decades without fire allow this tree to establish
itself in the shade of less shade-tolerant plants, like the pines.
Dense growths of young fir trees are a common sight under
older pines, under aspens and under older firs.

Red fir is found up to 10,000 feet on most trails in *Devils Postpile* quad, and is especially common on the Iron Creek Trail (Backpack Trail #3) and on the slopes between Reds Meadow and Mammoth Pass.

White fir (*Abies concolor*) is a lower-elevation relative of red fir. We can easily tell mature white fir from mature red fir by its gray-brown, as opposed to reddish, bark. In addition, white fir's cones are smaller than those of red fir, though they, too, disintegrate on the tree. Young fir trees are a bit more difficult to distinguish from each other. However, red-fir inner bark is invariably red, while that of white fir is not. Looking up through the crown of a white fir, we have a much more difficult time distinguishing individual needles and branchlets than we do on red fir, even on tall, old monarchs. Some people tell young white fir from young red fir by looking closely at their needles: longer, and twisted at the base in white fir, and two-ranked rather than coming out all around the twigs as in red fir.

A delicate, wispy subalpine species is mountain hemlock (*Tsuga mertensiana*). Found from about 9000 feet to timberline, it, like its associate whitebark pine, is often contorted into *krummholz* by the windy alpine environment.

The only plant mountain hemlock could possibly be confused with is red fir. However, when the fir's single needles break free of branches, they leave small, circular scars, whereas peglike projections are left when the hemlock's single needles are removed. Both have reddish bark, but that of hemlock is usually flakier. From a distance we see that mountain hemlock has a bent leader (tip) and a much more pendulous, drooping appearance to its branches than red fir, the limbs of which are more or less horizontal. Finally, mountain hemlock has persistent cones 1-3″ long that hang down, whereas red fir cones stick up.

Much of the mountain hemlock in our quad is near tree line and stunted, but stands of good-sized trees occur on the Beck Lakes loop above Johnston Meadow and just below Summit Meadow. This is *not* the poison-hemlock Socrates drank.

One broadleaf tree in the High Sierra is quaking aspen (*Populus tremuloides*), of the willow family. This tree is deciduous, losing all its leaves every autumn and growing a new crop in spring. Its round-ovate leaves tremble in the slightest breeze, hence the name. In the fall, before the leaves drop, they become a delicate lemon yellow, which turns the gullies and meadows that aspens inhabit into ribbons and seas of gold. The sight is particularly pleasing to easterners who miss the fall color of their native hardwood forests after coming west. Aspen bark is white-to-greenish, becoming gray and furrowed with age.

Although aspen ranges from Newfoundland to Alaska and into Mexico, the species is not abundant in the Sierra. We can usually expect to see them along streams and in open, wet meadows, where their moisture requirements are most readily met. Like lodgepole pine, quaking aspen is shade-intolerant and has easily disseminated seeds, so it, too, is a "pioneer" species which invades burns and meadows. Look for it above the North Fork of the San Joaquin on the trail from Devils Postpile to Twin Island Lakes, where it is especially well established.

The Fauna

OTHER GUIDES IN THIS SERIES have concentrated on the mammals of the High Sierra, but since birds are the most conspicuous animals in the high country—excepting, of course, mosquitos—let us here look at a few of the more abundant species of the Class *Aves*.

The most notable bird by far in *Devils Postpile* quadrangle is a member of the crow family: the Clark nutcracker *(Nucifraga columbiana)*. This bird is unmistakable. Usually heard before it is seen, it gives forth with a long, drawn-out, crowlike cry, "khr-a-a-a," as it swoops into the top of a whitebark pine tree to chip out a meal of pine nuts from the tree's closed cones (see *Flora*). The nutcracker's distinctive markings—gray body, black tail, and black wings with white patches—identify it in flight even at a distance. It is the only large bird so marked in the high country.

Not confined to a vegetarian diet, the Clark nutcracker also acts as a scavenger, consuming dead animals and campsite garbage, and as a predator, occasionally catching insects on the wing. It thus plays several roles in the timberline food web.

Everyone knows the robin *(Turdus migratorius)*, the most common member of the thrush family in North America. This bird is found from the tundra bordering the Arctic Ocean as far south as Guatemala at one time of the year or other. Most robins frequent *Devils Postpile* country during spring, summer and fall, though the author has sighted them high on Mammoth Mountain during a late winter blizzard.

A robin is not as brightly marked as a Clark nutcracker, but its brick-orange breast—lighter in the female—and its erect stance as it runs about a meadow searching for worms and insects are unmistakable. The clear, caroling songs of males during early season, by which they mark out their nesting territories, are a welcome sound to mountain travelers.

After leaving their nest of mud, grasses and small twigs in the forking branches of a tree, young, spotted-breasted robins group together with adults and work their way to lower elevations, where they feed largely on fruits and berries during the winter. Robins are probably one of the few animals that have become more abundant due to human changes on the face of the earth. Our clearing of deep forests and our cultivating of green lawns both increase this bird's habitat. In *Devils Postpile* quad, robins are most often seen in meadows and along streams where there are fruiting elderberry, currant and gooseberry bushes.

Another member of the thrush family, more often seen than heard, is the mountain bluebird *(Sialia currucoides)*. Unlike other bluebirds, the mountain bluebird is really a *blue* bird: it lacks the orange coloration of its lower elevation cousins.

Its commonest habitats are alpine fell-fields above timberline and meadows of the forest belt below 10,000 feet. We watch for mountain bluebirds hovering in the air and pursuing insects on the wing in the open country around Thousand Island Lake and at Marie Lakes, near the John Muir Trail. If the wind is still, we can hear their soft "churr" as they flit lightly about their open mountain habitat.

A third member of the thrush family we become familiar with while hiking the wooded paths of *Devils Postpile* quadrangle—this one more often heard than seen—is the hermit thrush *(Hylocichla guttata)*. Adult hermit thrushes have the characteristic spotted breast of the thrush family and a distinctive reddish tail which they slowly but continually cock up and let down. However, our commonest contact with this secretive bird is to hear the male's ethereal, flutelike note echoing through the forest, from early to midseason. His song consists of several distinct phrases, each introduced by a high, vibrant note, and is unlike any other sound in the mountains. Hermit thrushes winter below the deep-snow level on the west slope of the Sierra, but during the summer they can usually be heard along the Muir Trail near Upper Crater Meadow, among other places.

The dipper, or water ouzel *(Cinclus mexicanus),* is probably the most unusual bird the wilderness traveler will see in the Sierra. It is a permanent resident in and around mountain streams from the Aleutian Islands in Alaska all the way down to Panama. It remains all year round, as long as the water keeps flowing.

The dipper is the only bird one will see diving into a mountian stream and walking along the bottom. It is also the only songbird in the Sierra that commonly nests under waterfalls. This is the only avian of the High Sierra that sings year round. The chunky, slate-gray water ouzel was John Muir's favorite bird. *Devils Postpile* country visitors can expect to see water ouzels at Rainbow Falls and on Slide Creek near Hemlock Crossing, and indeed along most other permanent streams in the quadrangle.

After Clark nutcrackers and robins, one is probably more likely to see a dark-eyed junco *(Junco hyemalis, formerly called the Oregon junco)* than any other bird in the High Sierra—if we don't include campgrounds and thus exclude the raucous Steller jay.

Juncos are finches, and as such are primarily seed-eating birds, usually seen busily searching for food on the ground under trees and shrubs or out in open meadows. They are small birds with slate-gray heads, pinkish sides and striking white outer tail feathers, which flash in flight.

If one should suddenly be accosted by a loudly chirping junco—generally an extremely skittish bird—he can bet there is a well-lined, cuplike nest on the ground nearby which its owner would rather have remain unnoticed.

Dark-eyed juncoes are found from the lowest reaches of the San Joaquin River through all forest types in the quad to alpine fell fields, where at least some scattered dwarf willows exist for nest cover.

Another finch, and a bird of rather unusual habits, is the gray-crowned rosy finch *(Leucosticte tephrocotis),* denizen of the highest peaks and glaciers of the quadrangle. This bird is unlikely to be confused with any other, for only rarely do any other feathered creatures, much less a similar-looking one, enter their alpine habitat.

Small flocks of these reddish, sparrow-sized birds can be seen through most of the year, feeding on seeds and insects that have blown from lower, more productive ecosystems onto glaciers and snowfields. Only in the severest winter storms do they appear to retreat downslope; they can be found at any time during the summer season high on the snow and talus of the Minarets, Mt. Ritter and Banner Peak, the highest points in the quadrangle.

For many years, a veteran wilderness hiker may not associate a thin "seet seet tseetle tseet" in dense fir forest with any animal in particular. Then one day as the hiker is strolling from

77 Corral toward Sheep Crossing, a flattish, brown-and-white
bird about six inches long alights at the base of a large white
fir just off the trail and starts spiraling up the trunk. "Seet seet
tseetle tseet!" By golly! It's a brown creeper!

The high, wiry song of the brown creeper *(Certhia familiaris)*
is not often noticed by Sierra travelers, but it is nearly always
in the background when one is in heavy growth of red and white
fir and Jeffrey pine in *Devils Postpile* quadrangle.

This small, common, inconspicuous little bird feeds almost
exclusively on bark insects, using its tail as a brace in climbing
up tree trunks. Woodpeckers normally work up tree trunks also,
but they are much larger and noisier, and are usually predominantly black and white. Nuthatches are noisier and more colorful tree-stem foragers, and they usually go headfirst *down* a tree
rather than up it.

Thus that squeaking song you've heard all these years, and
that brown, mouselike creature flitting from tree trunk to tree
trunk, are effect and cause: the brown creeper.

To learn more about the birds found in *Devils Postpile* quadrangle, the interested reader is urged to peruse the bird guides
listed in the bibliography.

> "Where they [birds] most breed and haunt, I have
> observed
> The air is delicate."
>
>   Shakespeare

The Climate

CALIFORNIA'S WEATHER, and hence that of the Sierra Nevada, is governed by what goes on 2000 miles away, out over the Pacific Ocean. There, a permanent system of high pressure called the Pacific High moves north and south with the yearly march of the sun. In summer it is nearly due west of central California; in winter it lies off Baja.

When the Pacific High sits between the California coast and the subpolar low-pressure area in the Bering Sea during summer, it tends to keep the North Pacific's storms, bred in this low, from reaching the state. However, during the winter, the Pacific High is farther south, and also not as strong, while the subpolar low has increased in intensity. That's when storms move off the ocean over the land, and California gets rained on—or snowed on. Actually, it's not all that simple, but this brief sketch does help explain why about 53% of precipitation in *Devils Postpile* occurs in the winter, while only 3% comes during the summer, when most readers of this guide are likely to visit the mountains.

What about that 3%? This takes the form of short, summer-afternoon thunderstorms. When hot air from the Central Valley, or more rarely the Owens Valley, rises up the slopes of the Sierra, it cools at a rate of about 5.5°F per 1000 feet of altitude gain—the adiabatic rate of temperature change. In addition, the air over heat-radiating surfaces in the high country, such as an expanse of whitish granite, may rise convectively. Individually or together, these two phenomena cause the air to cool and drop its moisture. A thundershower is born. It "never rains in the Sierra in summer," but a cagoule or small tent is not that heavy—and wet sleeping bags aren't much fun.

Summer temperatures in the mountains vary with elevation.

Generally, the temperature in stable air decreases by about 3.6°F for every 1000-foot gain in elevation. So, a difference in temperature of 31°F can be expected between Miller Crossing (4567'), on the San Joaquin in the southwest corner of *Devils Postpile* quad, and the summit of Mt. Ritter (13,157') due to the difference in elevation alone. The average hiker is not likely to make this trip in one day, but the possibilities are dramatic. When we add the chilling effect of wind, a windless, 95° afternoon at Miller Crossing turns into an experience of 10° on Ritter, assuming a 25-mile-per-hour wind there. A windbreaker is another vital piece of summer paraphernalia.

One last comment on climate: solar radiation reaching the earth's surface increases with elevation. There may be four times as much ultraviolet at 14,000' as at sea level, and ultraviolet radiation causes sunburn. So visitors to the high country who burn easily, or who haven't got a good tan by the time they start living out in the sun, do well to liberally apply zinc oxide or some other good ultraviolet screen—such as those containing para-amino-benzoic acid—while here.

"At Christmas I no more desire a rose
Than wish a snow in May's newfangled mirth;
But like of each thing that in season grows."
                                                          Shakespeare

Backpackers

THERE ARE AS MANY REA- sons for backpacking as there are backpackers. One of the most frequently cited reasons has something to do with "getting away from it all," and this usually means going where there aren't many other people.

It has been claimed that the density of humanity in the mountains varies inversely with the *square of the distance* from a road, and with the *cube of the elevation* above the road. To this might be added a third exponent: the density of humanity also varies inversely with the *fourth power of a route's "off-trail-ness*," meaning the degree to which it is poorly marked or cross country. The hiker planning a trip in *Devils Postpile* can, by combining the trail descriptions and mileages in this volume, obtain a pretty fair idea of the probability of finding seclusion here.

The great increase in the use of the mountains for recreational pursuits has raised the question of just how many of us the land can handle. Overuse in *Devils Postpile* quad is evident in many places: the deeply eroded, multi-track pumice trails, especially near the Postpile; the nearly total lack of wood at the most popular campsites along the Muir Trail, such as Thousand Island Lake, Garnet Lake, Shadow Lake and Purple Lake; and accumulations of garbage and cans along Fish Creek. At various places in this guide, we recommend ways individual hikers can lessen their impact on the most heavily used areas—usually by camping someplace else and using a stove instead of wood fires. (In this second edition of the book, in fact, we have left out all mention of firewood at the campsites described, to hopefully lessen the overuse of this dwindling resource.) However, some

students and administrators of recreation areas foresee—in the
not-too-distant future—a need even to close popular sites for a
decade or more, so they can recover (as has been done, for
example, on some islands of the Boundary Waters Canoe Area
in Minnesota.) This procedure would allow, among other things,
compacted soil over suffocating tree roots to regain its porosity,
and human wastes to decay and be recycled.

As well, a permit system has been instituted to limit the
numbers of campers using those areas that have low capability
of absorbing footsteps, dishwater and feces. Both the National
Park Service and the U.S. Forest Service, which have the bulk
of the jurisdiction over our wilderness areas and other wild
places, have put together carefully thought-out rules that
should help all of us who love the mountains to enjoy them
without destroying their fragile beauty. We particularly encourage the use of only *existing* campsites greater than *100 feet*
from trails and water; the disposal of wash water and burial of
human wastes at *least 100 feet* from water, trails and campsites;
use of *stoves* for cooking, not wood, and much smaller camp-
fires; carrying out of *all* trash, *including* wet garbage; and res-
pect for the solitude of these mountain cathedrals. The wild
lands of North America are among the very last *hospitable*
natural places on earth that have not been completely abused
by humanity, technological as well as non-technological. It's
their last stand, and ours. It's up to us.

"In wildness is the preservation of the world."
Henry David Thoreau

The Trails

THE PROCLIVITY OF PEOPLE IN our convenience society to let their amazing bodies atrophy while doing everything "the easy way" won't get them very far in the Sierra backcountry. You walk—or, more rarely, ride stock—or else you get nowhere. This is refreshing for the body as well as the soul. On those steep, dusty switchbacks, and in those cold, wet fords, there is a feeling of accomplishment and of sensuous contact with mother earth which no manufactured vehicle can give. Even calves sore from a long descent, or heels blistered on that extra five miles, are a small price to pay for the good-tired feeling, "Here I am, and I'm pooped, but I did it myself."

But walking need not be exhausting. The attractions of *Devils Postpile* quadrangle are made accessible to a wide variety of hikers by a system of trails we can divide into three basic categories: backpack trails, lateral trails and day-hike trails.

Backpack Trails. Backpack trails vary in length and difficulty from the 8-km (5½-mi.) jaunt into Deer Lakes to the 40-km (25-mi.) marathon between Devils Postpile and Twin Island Lakes. There are also numerous weekenders into pristine alpine lakes from easily reached trailheads.

Lateral Trails. Four lateral trails are described in this volume. They connect scenic outposts, not normally visited by main-route travelers, to the backpack trails.

Day Hikes. A series of day hikes affords the visitor who is not inclined or able to take overnight trips quick access to scenic attractions that no one should miss seeing. Some trails may be walked in less than an hour, but remember, "this is not a place to make time but to spend it."

THE TRAILHEADS

Increasing vandalism to cars left at trailheads in the Sierra compels a few words of caution. Nothing of value should be left in sight in an unattended car, nor even in a locked glove compartment or trunk, especially overnight. Thieves are primarily after wallets and purses with their cash and credit cards. Carry them with you or leave them at home. A car should, of course, be locked, and it should be left in as unremote a spot as possible for long backpacks. Devils Postpile National Monument is much better in this regard than Agnew Meadows, where several dozen vehicles have been burglarized in one night.

Devils Postpile National Monument: 29 km (18 miles) west of U.S. 395 through Mammoth Lakes on State Highway 203.

Reds Meadow: 30 km (19 miles) west of U.S. 395 through Mammoth Lakes on State 203.

Agnew Meadows: 22 km (13½ miles) west of U.S. 395 through Mammoth Lakes on State 203.

Twin Lakes, Horseshoe Lake, Lake George: 10-13 km (6-8 miles) west of U.S. 395 through Mammoth Lakes. Where State Highway 203 turns off for Mammoth Mountain and Devils Postpile, continue straight.

Granite Creek Campground: 52 km (33 miles) northeast of the Bass Lake highway on road "434", 5S07 and 5S30 from the Pines, or 54 miles northeast of the town of South Fork on Forest Highway 100 and 5S30.

Glass Creek Trail: From the Crestview Highway Maintenance Station on U.S. 395, about 13 km (8 miles) north of the Mammoth Lakes junction, take the unmarked dirt road and bear *right, through* the campground, to road's end.

Trail Descriptions

(Distances are one-way, unless otherwise indicated.)

The route descriptions that follow often mention *ducks, cairns,* and *blazes.* A duck is one or several small rocks placed upon a larger rock in such a way that the placement is obviously not natural. A cairn is a number of small rocks made into a pile. A blaze is a mark at eye level on a tree trunk made by removing a small section of the bark with an axe.

To encourage the changeover to the metric system, distances in this section are given first in kilometers (km) and then in miles (mi.), except for short distances, which are given in meters.

DAY HIKE #1

Lake Barrett and T.J. Lake (1½ km, 1 mi. loop)

This short trip offers maximum high-country experience for a minimum of effort. It is recommended as a day hike—or even as an overnight backpack—for anyone who wants a beautiful but short hike.

The trail begins at the end of the road that runs through Lake George campground and along the shore of the lake. Our path crosses the bridged outlet of Lake George in a growth of mountain alders and then proceeds along the shore of the lake below

some cabins. After about 160 meters our signed route climbs
upward to the left on loose, layered, metamorphic rock, past
snowberry and pungent sagebrush. We cross a creek which has
been flowing on our right and continue ascending rather steeply on granite through mountain hemlock. Keeping to the left,
we arrive at Lake Barrett, which seems to be farther than the
¼ *mile* that the sign at Lake George indicates. Camping is poor
right on the lake but better on the bench up to the west.

The trail goes around the west side of Lake Barrett. Halfway
along the shore we turn right and climb slightly to the shores of
T.J. Lake. After such a brief walk from the road, one is amazed
at the wild beauty of the place. Crystal Crag soars in the west,
Mammoth Crest dominates the skyline to the south, and the
northwest shore is bounded by steep granite walls. Lodgepole
pines, silver pines and mountain hemlocks surround the lake,
and a small meadow at the upper end is covered by wildflowers
in mid season.

To complete the loop, we walk down the east side of the
outlet stream on an unmarked trail from T.J. Lake, where there
are some campsites. Dropping steeply through the forest, we
soon see Lake George below and Mammoth Mountain in the
distance. Just above a cabin on the lake, our route cuts to the
right and becomes a rough, wet fishermen's trail along the shore,
through a thicket of willows and alders. When we emerge from
the shrubbery, we are back where the trail begins to climb from
Lake George.

Right: Crystal Lake and Crystal Crag

DAY HIKE # 2

Lake George Campground to Crystal Lake (1½ km, 1 mi.)

Crystal Lake offers dramatic, high-country scenery and
solitude for a minimum expenditure of time and energy.

From the parking area across from the entrance to Lake
George Campground, we proceed up the well-defined trail that
begins there. This path takes us around the resort cabins above
Lake George. The trail may be lost in the tract, but it becomes
distinct again just below the top of the ridge directly behind
the cabins, where it begins a southward traverse. Here a sign
indicates that we are entering a wilderness area where motorized
traffic is prohibited. (The *actual* boundary of the John Muir
Wilderness is on Mammoth Crest, about 2½ km (1½ mi.) up
the trail.)

After climbing almost 1 km in deep pumice, we surmount
the ridge and see a panorama extending from Banner Peak and
Mt. Ritter in the west to Mammoth Mountain in the north and
Gold Mountain and Coldwater Canyon in the east.

From this viewpoint we continue to a signed fork where our
route veers left (SE) and another trail goes right (SW) to
Mammoth Crest and Deer Lakes. Our trail climbs over a hump
and then drops through mountain hemlock and lodgepole and
silver pine toward Crystal Lake, with Crystal Crag dominating
the landscape in the middle distance. The lake is set dramati-
cally at the base of Crystal Crag, towering 700 feet above.
Camping is possible on the east side and near the outlet, and
there is a nice sandy beach at the upper end of the lake.

DAY HIKE #3

Twin Lakes to Mammoth Mountain Summit (5½ km, 3½ mi.)

For vistas of the entire Mammoth Lakes basin and most of *Devils Postpile* quadrangle, the top of Mammoth Mountain is unexcelled. However, ski-area development on the mountain may turn some people off, and the hiker should be aware of nonesthetic roads and buildings at the top. (One is well-advised to dress warmly for this trek, because the west winds that roar almost constantly through Mammoth Pass can be devastating even on a warm summer day.)

Our trail leaves Twin Lakes campground at campsite 15W (also numbered T15) and climbs steeply through scattered lodgepole pines and red firs with some aspens, the latter grotesquely bent by the deep winter snows that make Mammoth Mountain one of California's best ski areas.

Several hundred feet above Twin Lakes the trail begins to level off, and we find some reddish porphyry, a fine-grained volcanic rock containing some clearly seen crystals. This rock is a characteristic relic of Mammoth Mountain's days as an active volcano. Approaching the Bottomless Pit—a natural arch formed by erosion through a lava flow—we switchback steeply up through a brushfield of manzanita, chinquapin, tobacco brush, rabbit brush and bitterbrush. Only occasional trees find a foothold in the shallow soil here. (Climbing in the Bottomless Pit is a danger because of the steepness and loose rocks not only to the climber but also to anyone down below at Twin Lakes, so the Forest Service has wisely closed the pit to hikers.) From here we take the route forking to the right and begin a rough, rocky ascent up the south side of the Dragons Back—the long, red, east flank of Mammoth Mountain—to Seven Lakes Point. When the sun is just right, one can see seven of the Mammoth Lakes from here—Mary, George, Mamie, Horseshoe, T.J. and Twin Lakes—as well as the White Mountains on the Nevada border, Crowley Lake in Long Valley, and Mammoth Crest.

From Seven Lakes Point we climb directly up the Dragons Back toward the summit. The few stands of hemlock, lodgepole and whitebark pine along the path offer dramatic relief from the nearly incessant winds blowing from the west through Mammoth Pass. This pass is the low point on the Sierra crest through which winter storms come and dump several hundred inches of snow each winter in the Mammoth Lakes area. This blanket of snow not only delights skiers but also accounts for the magnificent forest of nearly pure Jeffrey pine found east of Highway 395 between Crowley Lake and Mono Lake—an area that would otherwise consist largely of sagebrush scrub.

As our climb continues, we can see this forest to the northeast, as well as Mono Lake, Mono Craters and the lookout on Bald Mountain. We also get glimpses of the ski lifts and maintenance roads on the east slope of the mountain. A few hundred feet below the summit, the barely perceptible sand-and-pumice trail swings out to the south and switchbacks unnecessarily up the gentle slope. The few wildflowers able to contend with the sandblasting on this slope consist mostly of various buckwheats. The few whitebark pines that have been able to get a foothold—usually on the leeward side of a rock—are more horizontal than vertical.

From the true summit—a little rise to the northwest across the summit depression—one has a 360° panorama.

DAY HIKE # 4

Reds Meadow to Rainbow Falls (2 km, 1¼ mi.)

Walter A. Starr, Jr., author of the well-known *Starr's Guide to the John Muir Trail,* called Rainbow Falls "the most beautiful in the Sierra outside of Yosemite." To reach this gem on the San Joaquin Middle Fork, we park at the end of the spur road that goes west from the Reds Meadow road about 100 meters before the pack station, and start south down the well-worn trail.

After a short stroll under a cover of lodgepole pines, we cross the John Muir Trail—with Devils Postpile back to the right (NW)—and continue to Boundary Creek (log crossing). Shortly beyond the stream, the Fish Creek Trail (Backpack Trail # 6) continues on ahead, and we take the path to the right (W) for Rainbow Falls. The roar of the water fills our ears as we pass numerous vantage points for viewing and photographing the cascade from the cliffs above the river. Early-season afternoons seem to be the best time to behold the falls and its rainbow in full splendor.

From the most popular viewpoint a steep trail drops to the river, and swimming in the pool below the falls could blow one's mind. Dippers—also called water ouzels—nest on the moss-and-fern-covered walls beside the plunging water, and various aquatic invertebrates line the rocks around the pool. This place is a most delightful experience after several days' camping. Cameras and swimsuits are necessities on this hike.

DAY HIKE # 5

Horseshoe Lake-Reds Meadow Loop (19 km, 12 mi.)

This loop trip, which takes us over the Sierra crest twice, is very strenuous and only experienced hikers in good condition should attempt it. Most hikers will probably want to take one or the other branch of the loop down to Reds Meadow, there to be picked up by car or to hitch-hike out.

Past the end of the pavement and before the group campground at Horseshoe Lake, the Mammoth Pass Trail takes off uphill through deep pumice under lodgepole pines. There are occasional whitebark pines along the path, and in late summer we watch for Douglas squirrels chewing the cones apart to get the pine nuts.

Our route forks just below McLeod Lake, and we go left (SW) toward the lake. The return portion of this loop will bring us back to this junction from the right (NW). McLeod Lake is the domestic water supply for Mammoth Lakes, and "Pollution is prohibited." (Would that it were so easy elsewhere!) We skirt the north side of the lake through level pumice, climb a bit and then begin a barely perceptible descent—we have crossed the Sierra Crest. This saddle is not the highest part of the Sierra Nevada in this region—the Ritter Range is loftier—but nonetheless it is the dividing line between the eastern and western watersheds of the Sierra. The runoff west of this summit is part of the Great Valley drainage, which eventually runs into San Francisco Bay. The runoff to the east becomes part of the Owens River, most of which ends up—by unnatural means—in Los Angeles.

The trail begins to drop more steeply and to switchback down, and the forest becomes more mixed, as red fir, mountain hemlock and silver pine are added to the abundant lodgepole.

At the boundary of the John Muir Wilderness, a cutoff goes right (W) to Red Cones. We continue south toward Upper Crater Meadow, climb some, and then drop sharply to a junction with the John Muir Trail in the center of the meadow. Here we turn north onto the Muir Trail (Backpack Trail # 2) and walk 1½ km to Crater Meadow. Skirting this meadow, we climb on the Muir Trail part way up the more northern of the two Red Cones, and then we take off to the left (W) on an obscure, unmaintained path that drops across the lower portion of the cone. The trees are blazed, and litter of needles and cones collects where the trail provides a break in the pumice-and-cinder slope. (Another unmarked path leads into the meadow and then disappears.)

Beyond the meadow our route parallels Crater Creek. When the trail becomes hard to follow, we cross the stream and locate the path continuing down Crater Creek on the left side as it begins to cascade over vesiculated ("full of holes") lava. The trail soon begins to descend very steeply, and one is relieved to be going down to Reds Meadow on it rather than up. After 1 km of switchbacking down in deep, loose pumice, we begin to level off in an open forest of red fir, silver pine and Jeffrey pine. Large fire scars at the bases of some of the bigger trees attest to fire's part in keeping this stand open and parklike.

The trail swings north and crosses Crater Creek, quieter now, and Boundary Creek in close succession. The route here is level and often wet through red-fir forest. As is common in the whole area around Reds Meadow, there is a profusion of stock trails, especially in the soft pumice. We keep on what looks like the most heavily used route, leap several small streams not shown on the topo, and meet the rerouted John Muir Trail 200 meters south of the stables of Reds Meadow Pack Station. Here we can choose to terminate the trip by strolling to Reds Meadow.

To continue the loop back to Horseshoe Lake, we turn right onto the John Muir Trail and climb toward Mammoth Pass. A combination of high snowfall, springs and afternoon sunlight on this west-facing slope is at least partly responsible for the great size of the shrubs and trees along this part of the trail. There are bush lupines over 3 feet tall, gooseberry plants with berries more than ½ inch in diameter, and white firs to 5 feet in diameter. In late season it is not unusual to find intact fir cones on the ground along the way. Douglas squirrels cut them off while green, then collect them or chew them apart on the ground for their seeds. Normally, fir cones disintegrate on the tree and are not seen whole on the ground.

At the turnoff to Mammoth Pass 1½ km ahead, we fork left (E) and climb steeply through red fir toward the pass. Our route rises at a decreasing rate as we enter the broad expanse of the pass, and red fir begins to give way to lodgepole pine once again.

Back in Mammoth Pass, we note Mammoth Mountain in the north and Mammoth Crest in the south. A short distance beyond, we pass a weather-and snow-survey station used to gather data for predicting spring and summer runoff, and then we rejoin our earlier path at McLeod Lake for the short down-hill to Horseshoe Lake.

BACKPACK TRAIL # 1

John Muir Trail Northbound (32 km, 20 mi.)
(Devils Postpile National Monument to Donohue Pass)

This section of the John Muir Trail takes us along the east side of the Ritter Range through some of the most majestic scenery in the Sierra. Camping tends to be quite crowded on this route, and campsites are greatly overused at the more scenic spots, such as Shadow Lake.

We pick up the Muir Trail near a bridge about 300 meters south of the Devils Postpile National Monument parking lot and turn right, crossing the Middle Fork of the San Joaquin River on the bridge.

After the Summit Meadow/77 Corral Trail (Backpack Trail # 3) takes off to the left (S), we skirt the west edge of Soda Spring Meadow, where many Belding ground squirrels can be seen. (One can help the deteriorating trail situation here by staying where the trail has been closed and keeping to the left, rather than deepening any of the several ruts already here or making a new one.) We soon enter a stand of lodgepole pine and red fir and begin a steep ascent through deep, dusty pumice. At the top of this long traverse, the trail levels off, shortly before Minaret Creek, and passes a trail to Beck Lakes (Backpack Trail # 5). During high water Minaret Creek can usually be crossed above the ford on logs.

Our route, the Muir Trail, skirts the north side of Johnston Meadow, which has a magnificent display of wildflowers into mid season. Where we turn north from Johnston Meadow, the Minaret Lake Trail (Backpack Trail # 4) continues west up the

canyon of Minaret Creek, and our path resumes climbing in
dry, dusty pumice to tiny, meadow-fringed Trinity Lakes,
where an obscure fishermen's trail takes off west from our
route bound for Castle and Emily lakes.

Our Muir Trail continues northward, and after another
short ascent we skirt the west side of Gladys—or (on older
maps)—Vivian Lake. Here the trail affords views out over the
San Joaquin River canyon. To the west, the black igneous rocks
of Volcanic Ridge dominate the skyline, and to the east the
canyon walls drop away into the San Joaquin and rise on the
far side to red-topped San Joaquin Mountain and the distinctive
Two Teats.

From this viewpoint we descend to a saddle, and our path
leads around the east side of Rosalie Lake to good campsites
on the north shore. From this lake the trail drops through
forest via a long series of switchbacks to beautiful Shadow Lake,
once a true gem of the mountains. Camping here is now only
fair (and is restricted in some areas), due to crowds and site
degradation. This is one place along the John Muir Trail that is
really being worn out. The soil over tree roots around the lake
is being badly·compacted—which contributes to root disease
and tree death—and firewood is not to be found. Shadow Lake
may be a prime candidate for a "rest"—10 years without
campers, so that the land can recover. To conserve the fragile
beauty of Shadow Lake, this book recommends that travelers
not camp here but stop at Rosalie Lake or continue up Shadow
Creek, even though creekside campsites are suffering from
heavy camping pressure too.

After crossing the inlet of Shadow Lake, the Muir Trail joins
the Shadow Creek Trail (Backpack Trail # 7) and ascends west-

ward with it for 1½ km (1mi.) through Shadow Creek canyon
before branching north. This trail section suffers heavy use and
is likely to be dusty, particularly in late season. However, the
dust is behind us after the trail emerges from forest cover and
completes the 1100-foot climb from the Shadow Creek Trail
junction to the rocky ridge above Garnet Lake. This ridge is
an excellent place from which to appreciate the view of the
lake itself, Mt. Ritter and Banner Peak, and Mt. Davis in the
west. The traveler will also note the striking change in the
countryside. From the heavily timbered slopes of Shadow
Creek canyon, we have entered a landscape which, except for
scattered stands of stunted hemlock and lodgepole pine, is
predominantly glacially polished rock.

From this viewpoint the trail descends 500 feet to the outlet
of Garnet Lake. (A lateral leading to the River Trail branches
from our route just before the outlet of Garnet Lake. It passes
south of the rock outcrop beside the outlet and then drops
steeply through a notch into pine and hemlock forest, where it
switchbacks to a crossing of the Middle Fork and a junction
with the River Trail (Backpack Trail # 8.) Fair campsites may
be found near the outlet and on the north side of Garnet Lake.

Beyond the outlet of Garnet Lake, one should exercise care
in crossing the talus-covered 500-foot ridge that separates
Garnet and Thousand Island lakes. This section of trail, though
well-maintained, is rocky and can be dangerous when wet.
En route, the trail circles the east shore of dramatic Ruby Lake,
and then drops down past colorful Emerald Lake to the outlet
of Thousand Island Lake. The island-dotted lake's surface
reflects the imposing facade of Banner Peak and the more
sharply etched Mt. Ritter. Several exposed campsites (subject

to a great deal of wind coming down from Glacier Pass) may be
found around the outlet and on the north side of the lake,
where several streamlets run into Thousand Island Lake. Just
north of the lake's meadowy outlet, we pass the terminus of
the trails from Agnew Meadows (Backpack Trails # 8 and # 9)
and then climb upward away from the lake and onto a ridge
along a rerouted section of the Muir Trail. Along this ridge trail,
the hiker will discover a verdant growth of wildflowers including
lupine, elephant heads, sulfur flower, Mariposa lily, goldenrod,
fleabane, mountain aster, pussy paws and streptanthus.

The trail levels off for a while through lodgepole and hemlock, and then emerges from tree cover to the meadows and
ponds of Island Pass, where fairy shrimp and mountain frogs—
as well as mosquitoes—are abundant from early to mid season.
Camping is good here until the water stops flowing in mid
season. From Island Pass we drop steadily northwest through
forest cover and arrive at Rush Creek Forks, where camping
is good.

Our route passes the Rush Creek Trail (described in the
High Sierra Hiking Guide to *Mono Craters*) and then ascends
steeply through a thinning forest cover to the trail to Marie
Lakes (Lateral Trail # 4). From just south of this junction up
to Donohue Pass, the John Muir Trail crosses the southwest
corner of *Mono Craters* quadrangle. Leaving forest cover, the
trail winds up boulder-dotted, stream-laced meadows and then
climbs by rocky switchbacks to Donohue Pass on the crest of
the Sierra. Vantage points near this pass afford great views of
the Sierra crest, the Cathedral Range, the Ritter Range and
Lyell Canyon. (For the trail from here north, see the High
Sierra Hiking Guide to *Tuolumne Meadows.*)

Left: 1000 Island Lake, Banner Peak

BACKPACK TRAIL # 2

John Muir Trail Southbound (29 km, 18 mi.)
(Devils Postpile National Monument to Tully Hole)

The John Muir Trail southbound from Devils Postpile tours a fascinating portion of the Mammoth area's volcanic formations and then enters the granitic high country to the south. Our route leads from the main parking lot south toward Devils Postpile, past a large meadow on our right through which the Middle Fork of the San Joaquin River meanders. In mid season this meadow is a sea of lavender shooting stars, showy flowers that inhabit wet meadows throughout the quadrangle. At the south end of the meadow we step onto the famous John Muir Trail.

The well-packed pumice trail passes beneath the pillars of Devils Postpile, and several side trails lead to the top of the buttresses. Beyond the Postpile, the hiker encounters a profusion of tracks in the easily disturbed pumice. One should stay on the most heavily used and blazed route, and watch for signs. The trail is gently rolling here, through a forest of lodgepole pine, red fir and Jeffrey pine, with few vistas to relieve the monotony of the trees. We pass a lateral trail that follows the Middle Fork of the San Joaquin to Rainbow Falls, and then, after crossing a steam densely lined with mountain alder, we pass three more lateral trails in succession—to Rainbow Falls, Reds Meadow Campground and Bathhouse, and Reds Meadow Resort, respectively. In recent years, this portion of the John Muir Trail has been rerouted around the Reds Meadow Area, so that it no longer passes through it.

Swinging around Reds Meadow, we cross a score of stock

trails, eroded deeply into the pumice, which lead south from the pack station toward Rainbow Falls, the Red Cones and Cascade Valley. This trail situation can be quite confusing, but careful attention to the quite adequate signing here should keep one on the correct track. We meet, follow south for about 50 meters, and then leave the Fish Creek Trail to begin a long ascent out of the Middle Fork canyon. After 1 km of gentle climbing through red-fir forest, we pass another lateral to Reds Meadow Hot Springs. Then, climbing steadily upward in pumice, we get occasional glimpses of Mt. Ritter and the Minarets to the west through a heavy growth of fir trees. Mixed in here with red fir is white fir, distinguished by its gray-brown, as opposed to reddish, bark. The ground cover here is rather sparse, probably due to heavy shade and to the dryness of the pumice soil; happily, the yellow western wallflower is abundant all along the trail in midseason.

After we go by the Mammoth Pass Trail junction, our route climbs less steeply, and we begin to see lodgepole and silver pines among the red firs. Leveling off and then dropping through deep pumice, we catch previews of the Red Cones off to the southwest and soon pass a signed trail to the summit of the more northern of the two. (From the top of this cone there is a fine panorama of Mammoth Mountain, the Ritter Range and the canyon of the Middle Fork.) Our route continues past other trails that lead to Mammoth Pass and Reds Meadow, and descends into Crater Meadow, where there are several good campsites, covered in early season by a dense cloud of mosquitos. In early season the presence of these pests is compensated for by the abundance of flowers—shooting stars, pussy paws and lupine being especially plentiful.

From Crater Meadow the Muir Trail climbs south, crosses a divide, and drops into Upper Crater Meadow, where the deeply rutted trail ought to be rerouted around the fragile meadow soon. Here Belding ground squirrels keep the soil loose with their burrowing, and lodgepole pines are invading the grasses along the meadow's edge. A long, gentle climb takes us through another long meadow where we can see The Thumb to the north. A profusion of streamlets and springs lines this section of the trail in early season, so there is the possibility of camping here when the more popular sites along the trail are taken. Along this stretch we often hear the raucous calls of Clark nutcrackers, as well as the ethereal tune of the hermit thrush. As we begin to drop down toward Deer Creek on a dry, south-facing slope through sagebrush, Indian paintbrush, chinquapin, manzanita and gooseberry, we get our first views of Fish Valley and the Silver Divide ahead.

Camping is good at Deer Creek. Leaving here, one is wise to carry water for the next three miles, which are dry, hot, dusty, and up. During late season, one might not encounter water again until Duck Creek, 8 uphill kilometers ahead. On this long traverse through open lodgepole-pine forest above Fish Valley, the footing ranges from pumice to granite sand, and we have increasingly revealing views up glaciated, U-shaped Cascade Valley and to the Silver Divide. Another pine we begin to encounter as we gain elevation is whitebark pine, *the* subalpine tree of the Sierra. (About halfway between Deer and Duck creeks we leave *Devils Postpile* quadrangle and enter the southeast corner of *Mt. Morrison.*)

Duck Creek is a reliable source of water along this dry section of the Muir Trail, and it offers limited camping even though it's quite rocky and exposed. Switchbacks up the east slope beyond Duck Creek lead us to the trail to Duck Lake, which lies 1½ km upstream. Past the junction, our route swings south, rounds a rocky granite shoulder, and veers eastward to the several good campsites near the outlet of Purple Lake. The partly timbered, rocky shoreline gives way to meadow at the northeast end of the lake, and cliffs above this meadow give the lake its name: they have a rosy tint during the day but often turn purple and violet around sunset.

In mid season, hikers who seek more solitude than Purple Lake generally affords may want to pound out the 3 additional kilometers to Lake Virginia. After a steep, switchbacking climb above Purple Lake, the trail levels out across a broad pass. Here, what geologists call a "contact" is evident on the wall south of the pass, with dark metamorphic rock to the east and lighter granite to the west. From the pass we descend through subalpine forest of whitebark pine, interspersed with alpine fell fields, to the exposed campsites on Lake Virginia, where wildflower and bird shows make up for any inconvenience. Before the soggy meadows dry out, they support the blossoming of alpine laurel, red heather, cinquefoil and scrub willow. Birds to listen and watch for include robins, mountain chickadees, gray-crowned rosy finches, Brewer's blackbirds, Clark nutcrackers and spotted sandpipers, as well as an occasional California gull on the lake itself. Belding ground squirrels in the meadows, and marmots and conies in the talus, are the conspicuous furbearers at this excellent lake.

Where the John Muir Trail crosses the inlet at the north end of the lake, it is underwater in early season, and this place has to be forded. Our route leaves Lake Virginia and soon begins to drop toward Tully Hole, at first gently and then in steep switchbacks down a ridge between two streamlets. From the lake's outlet and from the trail down into Tully Hole, the fabulous vistas of the Silver Divide and Mt. Izaak Walton add to the immense beauty of this area. The meadows in Tully Hole are rampant with wildflower color: forget-me-not, buckwheat, wallflower, wild strawberry, pennyroyal and thistle. There is good camping, though mosquitoey in early season, in the northwest corner of the meadow, at the junction (hard to see) with the trail to McGee Pass. (From Tully Hole the Muir Trail continues down Fish Creek as described in the High Sierra Hiking Guide to *Mt. Abbot.*)

BACKPACK TRAIL #3

Devils Postpile to Twin Island Lakes (40 km, 25 mi.)

This trail over the Ritter Range follows a portion of the old Mammoth Trail, which prospectors and stockmen used in the late 19th century to cross the mountains between Clover Meadow and Reds Meadow. It offers the easiest crossing to the little used North Fork country.

To get on the trail, we walk through the meadow south of the parking lot at Devils Postpile National Monument and turn right to cross the bridge over the Middle Fork of the San Joaquin River. For a few meters we are on the famous John Muir Trail, linking Yosemite and Mt. Whitney. Then we turn south at the King Creek/Clover Meadow Trail junction and begin a climb through lodgepole pine in deep, dusty pumice. Along this ascent we have a nice overview across the San

Joaquin to the andesite buttresses that formed when molten lava cooled to form long, straight-sided columns about 630,000 years ago. After the first switchback, Mammoth Mountain and the Red Cones come into sight through scattered red and white fir, mixed with silver pine. Soon after leaving the monument and entering Inyo National Forest, we descend through a forest of scattered firs and Jeffrey pines to King Creek. Take a whiff of the strongly scented bark of a large Jeffrey pine: is it vanilla or root beer?

In early and midseason the observant hiker is likely to see the brilliant red snow plant here. A member of the wintergreen family, it is a flowering plant that lacks chlorophyll and hence cannot carry on photosynthesis. It lives on dead organic matter in the soil.

King Creek offers good camping and yields up small rainbow trout (6-8″) to fishermen. An easy crossing can be made on logs 30 meters downstream below the ford; then the uphill grind to Summit Meadow begins. We soon leave the fairly dense cover of trees and come out onto a dry slope covered with manzanita and huckleberry oak. While stopping for a breather, the hiker has a panoramic vista to the east and south, from Mammoth Mountain to the Silver Divide. Wild strawberries, Indian paintbrush and mountain pride blanket the ground here.

From the dry slope we begin climbing steeply into dense mountain hemlock as the Minarets appear in the north. About ½ kilometer below Summit Meadow, the Summit Meadow cutoff to upper King Creek leads off to the right. The topo map erroneously shows this junction at Summit Meadow itself. Summit Meadow, which was used for summer sheep grazing until the year 1963, has since become almost totally covered with lodgepole pine, a pioneer species which at this elevation in the Sierra is the next step in ecological succession (see the chapter "Flora"). The trampling and grazing of sheep apparently kept the meadow from turning into forest while grazing continued, but when the Forest Service limited sheepherding to the west side of the North Fork of the San Joaquin, the broken ground here in the meadow was an ideal place for seeds from the surrounding lodgepole-pine forest to germinate and carry on the natural process of succession.

Climbing beyond Summit Meadow—which is neither a meadow nor at the summit—we enter a dense stand of lodgepole pine and red fir, and after entering Sierra National Forest at the top of Granite Stairway, we drop steadily on rocky granite footing to the base of Granite Stairway and leave Inyo's pumice behind. Groundsel, golden brodiaea and scarlet penstemon delight the eye as we level off and arrive at Stairway Creek, where there is good camping about 50 meters upstream. Dry, late-season conditions come sooner at these lower elevations, so there are fewer mosquitos here than there are higher up. We continue downhill to Lower Stairway Meadow, which in mid season is covered with nodding lavender shooting stars. Some of the common summer birds seen along the trail at this elevation are brown creepers, white-and red-breasted nuthatches, kinglets and nest-robbing Steller jays.

After a short climb out of Lower Stairway Meadow, the trail levels off through red-fir and lodgepole-pine forest, and we get our first glimpses of the Isberg Pass country to the northwest.

Soon, however, our route begins a steep, switchbacking descent into Cargyle Meadow, down the northwest slope of a glacial moraine which is a riot of wildflower color in mid season. Numerous small springs dotting the hillside nourish forget-me-not, elderberry, pennyroyal, Indian painbrush, cranesbill, lupine, monkey flower and scrub willow. Cargyle Meadow, which we circle to the south before crossing the East Fork of Cargyle Creek, is itself a sea of blooms—shooting star, knotweed, wild strawberry and Labrador tea. On the north side of Cargyle Meadow, polished granite bedrock evinces the scraping power of the glaciers that passed here over 10,000 years ago.

Our route crosses the creek, where camping is fair, then climbs over a rise and drops to Corral Meadow, also called 77 Corral. During the drought of 1877, this was one of the pastures in the Sierra heavily used by sheepmen—hence the signed designation *77 Corral.* From 77 Corral, where there are several little-used campsites, trails lead to Iron Lake, Granite Creek Campground (Backpack Trail #12) and Iron Creek. We proceed northwest toward Iron Creek, 5 miles away. The Iron Creek Trail is well-maintained and marked by many unnecessary ducks. It climbs almost imperceptibly through open forest to fair campsites on Cargyle Creek.

Continuing upward more steeply onto a dry, west-facing slope, we begin to encounter scattered sagebrush among the trees. Then we break out into Headquarters Meadow, where sagebrush and buckbrush are being invaded by lodgepole pine and even red fir. This seems unusual, since red fir is not generally observed as a pioneer species in meadow and brushfield succession. Because the vegetation is short, we have a fine vista from here to the south, where the canyons of the North and Middle forks of the San Joaquin River join below Junction Bluffs.

Our path passes through a stand of red fir and then emerges into Earthquake Meadow, where numerous signs mark a trail junction. A 3-km lateral leads southwest to Snake Meadow; an unmaintained route (not shown on the topo map) to Strobe Lake heads northeast; and our route continues northwest toward Iron Creek. Leaving Earthquake Meadow, we descend gently through open white-fir forest with a buckbrush and bush-chinquapin understory. After a level segment, the trail begins ascending across a large meadow that slopes away in the west toward the North Fork of the San Joaquin. Here one may ponder the picturesque, snow-bent aspen, which are especially beautiful in fall after their leaves have turned golden yellow. They have a fragile beauty that is singularly welcome among the faded browns of autumn.

Beyond this unnamed meadow, our well-blazed trail rolls along for a mile in a varied forest and then drops sharply down to Iron Creek. Where it levels off there is good camping in a stand of Jeffrey pine, white fir, Sierra juniper and lodgepole pine. Before the trail leaves this tree cover along Iron Creek and plunges down to the North Fork of the San Joaquin, a very faint fishermen's trail to the river and the gaging station (see Lateral Trail # 1) crosses to the south side of Iron Creek. We continue on the main trail and descend steeply across a dry, southwest-facing slope covered with a dense growth of huckleberry oak, sagebrush and manzanita. Then we cross a loose talus slide of sharp metamorphic rocks, which could be dangerous, particularly when wetted by rain or snowmelt. After this quick drop, we finally arrive at the North Fork and begin the upriver stretch of our route. First we ascend very gently about ¾ km through a series of wet meadows inhabited by willows, tall sedges and other water-tolerant species such as red dogwood and aspen, to Dike Creek. Here there is an "Improved" campsite just below a beautiful cascade that feeds a series of pools on the river.

A short, rocky climb from Dike Creek takes us around a rocky shoulder. This shoulder blocks the river from our view, but up and down the valley we can see the typical U-shaped cross section of a glaciated canyon. Then the trail cuts back to the river and crosses over to the west side. (The trail re-crosses to the east side of the river at Hemlock Crossing, about 100 meters upstream. To avoid two difficult crossings during high water, one can scramble along the rocks above the river on the east side, to rejoin the trail farther ahead at Hemlock Crossing.) Crossing the North Fork to the west side, we enter a stand of lodgepole pine and red fir, where a sign tells us that we are now in the Minarets Wilderness. Hopefully, wilderness status will someday be accorded to the area south of here, too, linking the John Muir and Minarets wilderness areas together and frustrating any plans to destroy this pristine country with a trans-Sierra highway.

Going through the campsite here we pass the trail to Clover Meadow Guard Station and Granite Creek Campground (Backpack Trail # 11), and arrive at Hemlock Crossing. Here the North Fork breaks through the beds of westward-dipping strata it has been paralleling, and plunges into a wide pool—ideal for swimming late in the season, when the water level is lower and the temperature higher. This is an excellent place to camp. Strangely, there are no hemlocks right at Hemlock Crossing,

but there are 3 or 4 downstream, where the trail to Iron Creek
crosses the river. The ford is rocky and cold.

Our route as we leave Hemlock Crossing for Twin Island
Lakes is the one shown *east* of Slide Creek on the topo map.
We climb above the stream past penstemon, lupine, azalea and
paintbrush, while below us water ouzels bounce up and down
on rocks in the creek.

The trail several times ascends and levels off over a series of
benches as we climb up the east wall of the canyon. This steplike relief is largely due to underlying beds of rock, which have
differential resistance to erosion. The topography is in turn
responsible for the collection of rain and snowmelt water into
the ponds we see in various stages of ecological succession—
from open water to meadow to forest—for the next 3 km along
the trail. Mosquitoes, as a consequence, are dense all along the
route from early to mid season. Stands of lodgepole pine,
Jeffrey pine and red fir are interspersed with brushy openings
of sagebrush, huckleberry oak and manzanita. Then we pass
through dusty "Lonesome Joe Camp" and climb to the easy
crossing of Slide Creek.

Here we enter what is shown on the map as "Stevenson
Meadow," but is actually a series of wet meadows separated by
stands of trees. The wildflower show compares with any in the
Sierra: shooting star, monkey flower, penstemon, corn lily,
delphinium, knotweed, groundsel, forget-me-not and mountain
aster are especially evident in mid season. The peak of bloom-
ing seems to coincide with the peak of mosquitoes, and insect
repellent is essential at this time of year. As the trail leaves
Stevenson Meadow and climbs west above the cascading North
Fork, we have better views ahead of the ridge on the southeast

boundary of Yosemite National Park, topped by Electra and Rodgers peaks.

Just past the roaring junction with Bench Canyon, the North Fork veers northeast, and there is excellent camping here in a heavy growth of lodgepole, fir and hemlock. From this point on to Twin Island Lakes, the trail becomes increasingly difficult to follow, and only experienced hikers should continue. The Forest Service no longer maintains the trail beyond Stevenson Meadow. The route is often over glacially polished rock, and there are only occasional ducks to mark the path. Where there is vegetation, the trail is poorly blazed and often overgrown with willows and shrubs. However, the rewards in solitude and scenic beauty which lie ahead are well worth the effort.

Our route climbs away from the river before traversing back toward it, at a higher elevation. Then we drop slightly into a meadow, the North Fork flowing rather placidly on our left. For the next 3 km, the trail alternately leads away from the North Fork across meadows and snowmelt streams and climbs back toward the river on glacially polished basaltic rock. Occasional stands of red fir and lodgepole pine offer sheltered and definitely uncrowded camping. Where there are trees along the trail, the blazes are usually either grown over or nonexistent, so we have to rely on ducks to find the route.

As the trail approaches the stream draining Ritter Lakes and Lake Catherine, it veers east away from the North Fork into a long sagebrush-and-grass meadow. When the falls of this stream finally come into sight, the hiker should avoid the indicated crossing on the topo map, because it crosses the stream where it is split into several channels covered with dense brush, and fording is very difficult here in early and mid season.

A better choice is to go either lower, near the river, or higher, near the falls. Once past this obstacle, the experienced hiker should be able to pick out the ducked route to Glacier Pass and to follow it up to the base of the cliffs, where it strikes eastward. The route to Twin Island Lakes leaves cross country from this point, heading almost due west and somewhat upward through the gap that lies just east of the more northern and larger of the Twin Island Lakes. Camping at the larger lake is best either near the inlet on the north end or on a point of the eastern shore opposite the islands.

Not many travelers get to Twin Island Lakes or to the lakes higher up the North Fork watershed. Solitude reigns. Among the few sounds striking the alpine listener's ear are the raucous calls of the ubiquitous Clark nutcracker, the squeaking of a cony and the rustling of breezes through stunted whitebark pine. Cinquefoil, penstemon, mountain aster and red heather highlight the glacially eroded landscape with spots of color. The water is clear and cold. And the alpenglow on Mt. Davis and other, unnamed peaks to the north is rarely excelled. The way to Twin Island Lakes is difficult, but the rewards are great.

BACKPACK TRAIL # 4

Devils Postpile to Minaret Lake (11 km, 7 mi.)

Minaret Lake affords some of the finest closeups of the stark and jagged Minarets that can be had on a weekend trip. To get there, we take the John Muir Trail northbound (Backpack Trail # 1) from Devils Postpile National Monument to Johnston Meadow. Then, where the Muir Trail turns north, we continue upstream to the west. Our trail climbs in pumice through a forest of red fir, silver pine, lodgepole pine and mountain hemlock, and then breaks out onto a granite slope, where it switchbacks up beside the cascades of Minaret Creek. As we labor up the switchbacks, we get increasingly better views of the marvelous Minarets.

After leveling out, our path passes an obscure lateral to Minaret Mine (operated 1928-1930). Just north of here is a moderately warm pond with good swimming in late season. From here, ¾ km of level walking beside the meandering stream brings us to good campsites beside the creek. The silent early-morning riser is apt to see browsing Inyo mule deer in these meadows. From the campsites, a steep, rocky ascent takes us through the last timber stands before laboring up some rocky switchbacks to Minaret Lake. Good campsites dot the northern shore.

Settled beside this dramatic lake, one looks with awe on the towering array of arêtes to the south and west. Clockwise, from the south, the prominent Minarets are Riegelhuth, Pridham, Kehrlein, Ken and Clyde. Pridham Minaret has a Class 2 route, suitable for the unroped climber (see *Mountaineers Guide to the High Sierra*). These knife-edge ridges are remnants of ancestral mountains that existed more than one hundred million years before the present Sierra was uplifted. Glacial plucking at their bases and frost wedging in their cracks and joints have determined their striking relief. Minaret Lake is often used as a base camp for "technical" climbing in the Minarets.

BACKPACK TRAIL # 5

Devils Postpile to Beck Lakes (29 km, 18 mi.)

This loop trip takes us in a long, clockwise circle from Devils Postpile National Monument to King Creek, Fern Lake, Beck Cabin and Beck Lakes, and back again to the Postpile. It tours a little-visited area surprisingly close to the road. The loop may be walked in the other direction, but doing it clockwise avoids 8 uphill kilometers of deep pumice between the Postpile and Beck Cabin.

The first 10 km of this trail, to the cutoff below Summit Meadow, are described in Backpack Trail # 3. Just before Summit Meadow, we leave the Twin Island Lakes Trail and head north for Beck Lakes. After the long haul from King Creek, this trail is a welcome gentle downhill stretch through swales of willow, elderberry and corn lily, and dense stands of mountain hemlock. After ¾ km we come to the lateral to Fern Lake. This short trail follows the south bank of the outlet stream to good campsites on the lakeshore. There is a nice beach on the Southwest corner of the lake.

Continuing beyond the Fern Lake lateral, we pass several wet meadows and ponds and then descend to the junction of King Creek and the outlet stream of Anona Lake. We cross the several branches of Anona Lake outlet fairly easily, but then the path becomes very difficult to follow where it swings up to the west before switchbacking across the open metamorphic slope west of cascading King Creek. Watch for blazes on the scattered lodgepoles. We climb steeply above King Creek, with views back toward Mammoth Crest and the Silver Divide, and then drop to a cold ford, which is much easier to negotiate in

Left: Minaret Lake

late season when the water is low. Our route soon intersects
the Holcomb Lake Trail (Lateral Trail # 2) at a mosquito-
infested meadow, so we hurry on to Beck Cabin, built by an
early prospector in this area and now dilapidated.

The Beck Lakes Trail takes off to the north at a sign near
the cabin and crosses numerous wet meadows, dotted with
sweet-scented Labrador tea and pink-bloomed bog laurel, on
its way to Superior Lake. Several campsites near the lake's
inlet and outlet offer fair-to-good camping. Beyond Superior
Lake the path is difficult to follow in early season, due to deep
snows on this shady, northeast slope. It is best to stay left of
the stream as the route skirts the south side of a meadow above
Superior Lake and ascends through open stands of mountain
hemlock and wet, grassy meadows.

Our path crosses the outlet stream of the lower lake just
above a grove of mountain hemlock, and from the ford we
follow the ducked route to Lower Beck Lake. Camping is stark
but scenic on the north shore of the lower lake and south of
the outlet. A faint rocky trail along the north side of the lower
lake leads to Upper Beck Lake, which is quite barren save for
some stunted alpine vegetation. Red-tinted green algae color
lingering snowbanks here throughout the summer.

To complete our loop, we backtrack to Beck Cabin and then
climb east across a slope dotted with silver pine, red fir and
prostrate manzanita. The dramatic vista ahead includes the
Silver Divide, the Middle Fork San Joaquin canyon and Snow
Canyon, and looking back we have a last glimpse of Iron Mountain and the south end of the Ritter Range. We cross the crest
of the ridge we've been climbing, drop slightly to a wet meadow, and then climb once again through mixed forest.

After this short, steep ascent, the trail to the Postpile is generally downhill in ever-deepening, dry, dusty pumice. The hiker
now appreciates the direction of this loop.

   Long switchbacks soon bring us out above Johnston Lake
and Johnston Meadow, about 600 feet below. On this relatively
cool and shady northeast slope, the tree cover is made up of
shade-tolerant red fir and mountain hemlock. On this steep
slope the typical tree trunk has a curve near the ground. Snow
creeping downslope bent the trees as seedlings and saplings.
After they grew large enough to resist this force and remain
upright during the winter, the deformed bases remained.

   After a long, steep descent, we leave the Minarets Wilderness,
and meet the Muir Trail, which we follow back to Devils Postpile National Monument.

BACKPACK TRAIL # 6

Reds Meadow to Cascade Valley (30 km, 19 mi.)

   The Fish Creek-Cascade Valley Trail is the primary pack-
train route out of Reds Meadow, and it tends to be crowded
and dusty. However, it leads to good fishing and to a glaciated
canyon that to some eyes resembles Little Yosemite Valley.

   We walk south from the parking lot near Reds Meadow, as
described in Day Hike # 4, but at the Rainbow Falls turnoff
we continue south on the Fish Creek Trail, under a canopy of
pine and fir. Compared to most of the trails in the quadrangle,
this one passes through areas of relatively low elevation, where
we see plants not encountered in the Devils Postpile high country, such as incense-cedar and black oak. The path is nearly
level here, but wide and deep through dusty, easily disturbed

pumice. Then we come to Crater Creek, and stroll along with refreshing riparian vegetation on our left and dry pine forest on our right.

The crossing of Crater Creek is best made about 10 meters upstream on two logs in a dense growth of alder. Continuing beyond the crossing, one notices again the great difference in environments between streamside and dry hillside. Along the creek are dense growths of alder, bracken, willow and currant, and such wildflowers as orange Sierra lily, 6-foot-tall cow parsnip and both pink and yellow monkey flowers. Out in the pumice, however, away from the immediate vicinity of the stream, there are scattered Jeffrey pines and red and white firs, and manzanita is the predominant shrub. After the trail crosses an unnamed stream, we come onto a granite slope which in early season is overrun with hundreds of snowmelt rills. This slope is an excellent example of what the ecologist calls "primary succession": a new surface, never covered by plant life previously, is being overlaid with vegetation. Meltwater from winter snows and weathered rock are allowing alders, willows and other pioneer plants to get a shallow foothold on the otherwise bare granite (see the chapter "Flora"). The trail is blasted out of the granite in places; we have left the pumice behind.

Near the ford of Cold Creek is good camping. From here our route climbs first through aspen and then through a stand of large Jeffrey pine, incense-cedar and white fir, with a few California black oaks scattered around. At the end of this climb, we cross a divide and begin dropping, at first gently and then steeply down switchbacks, into Fish Valley. Silver Creek is visible south across the canyon. Lower-elevation black oak and incense-cedar are becoming more frequent as we descend, and mosquitoes are rare on this dry, south-facing slope. Two thirds of the way down, the trail grades into a long, gentle, eastward traverse, passes the washed-out and abandoned bridge site, and ends at Island Crossing. There is a heavily used fishermen's camp here. More secluded accommodations can be found both upstream and downstream, where fallen trees offer dry crossings.

As we head up Fish Valley, open Jeffrey-pine groves with sagebrush and lupine underneath alternate with dense stands of white fir and incense-cedar. About 2¼ km upstream, Fish Creek makes a sharp bend north, and our path continues beside Shark-tooth Creek through cool, green stands of alder, azalea, elder-berry, currant and gooseberry. In early season the fragrance of swamp onion wrinkles the nose of the hiker who steps on it when leaving the trail to skirt numerous flooded spots. We pass several heavily used packer campsites along the stream, go by the Sharktooth Trail junction, and then cross Sharktooth Creek to Iva Bell Camp, which is even more heavily used and is not uncommonly littered with dog-food cans and beer cans.

From Iva Bell Camp we make a short, steep climb over a chaparral-covered ridge and then descend to Fish Creek again. The steam drops fast here between glacially polished walls of granite, and the trail occasionally climbs around rock outcrops on its way to Second Crossing. In mid season this stretch of trail is a riot of wildflower blooms: paintbrush, penstemon, forget-me-not, wallflower, gilia and Mariposa lily are all evident. Fording at Second Crossing is easy only in late season. Above Second Crossing, Jeffrey pine and juniper alternate with aspen and lodgepole in the drier, rockier spots, while black cotton-wood and aspen line the stream. Many lovely pools offer fine opportunities for both swimming and fishing along this section

of the creek. At the outlet stream of middle Lost Keys Lake we leave *Devils Postpile* quad and enter *Mt. Morrison.* After 1½ km our path crosses the several distributaries of Duck Creek, then climbs south over a little ridge before finally dropping to the flats of Cascade Valley.

Cascade Valley is a steep-sided, flat-bottomed valley which was gouged out by glaciers originating at the Sierra crest over 10,000 years ago. The valley gets its name from the cascades of tributary streams, such as Purple Creek, Long Canyon and Minnow Creek, which were left hanging when the glacier deepened the main valley more than the side canyons. Fish Creek meanders here in what was once possibly the bed of a glacial lake, formed behind a recessional moraine of the Fish Creek glacier. As we stroll through the lodgepole pine stands interspersed with meadows, we see the rare black-backed three-toed woodpecker, as well as the commoner robin, the dark-eyed junco, and the scolding winter wren.

Numerous pack-train trips terminate in Cascade Valley; it is a popular stopping point for travelers passing through, and in summer there is a Forest Service wilderness ranger near Purple Creek, so one is seldom alone in this place—and that's another way that it resembles Little Yosemite Valley. After the Minnow Creek Trail leaves our path, and the steep path to Purple Lake takes off to the north, our Fish Creek Trail continues upstream 2 km to Third Crossing. (This description is continued in the High Sierra Hiking Guide to *Mt. Abbot.*)

Left: Fish Creek

BACKPACK TRAIL # 7

Agnew Meadows to Ediza Lake (10 km, 6½ mi.)

This trail leads to the spectacular Ritter Range, capped by
Banner Peak, Mt. Ritter and the Minarets. Some say the alpine
beauty of all Sierra lakes culminates at Ediza Lake, where amid
towering evidences of glacial and volcanic action, the visitor
can readily appreciate the colossal forces that shaped these
natural landforms. The alpine meadows at the southeast end
of Ediza Lake are often used as base-camp sites by mountain
climbers on the way to ascend the Minarets, Mt. Ritter and
Banner Peak. Scaling most of these peaks requires technical
rock-climbing experience, and hikers who have not had such
experience should not attempt them without the guidance of
capable climbers.

From the trailhead north of Agnew Meadows Pack Station,
the trail passes south of a fenced meadow, surmounts a small
ridge covered by red fir and lodgepole pine, and descends
toward the San Joaquin River. Soon we skirt the northeast
side of lily-padded Olaine Lake, and then in a couple of hundred yards come to the Shadow Lake Trail, on which we turn
left. On this trail we approach the river in a stand of quaking aspen. The ford here is usually passable, but during high
water, one can make a dry crossing by finding fallen logs up-
or downstream from the stock crossing.

The trail up the west side of the canyon is rocky but well-
maintained. This path rises steeply for 800 feet along juniper-
dotted switchbacks, and the hiker is rewarded by excellent
views of cascading Shadow Creek as it falls from the lip of
Shadow Lake's basin. Our arrival at lovely Shadow Lake is

Right: Shadow Lake and the Ritter Range

through a notch in the metamorphic rocks, where we have a water-level view of the lake, with the grand Ritter Range as a backdrop. Fair campsites may be found around the lake, but they are being destroyed by overuse, and the author strongly discourages camping here, to delay the demise of the lake.

From Shadow Lake the trail ascends near cascading Shadow Creek. Several waterfalls along the stream invite the traveler to stop and rest. There are deep holes for fishing or for swimming (in late season). For 2½ km above the inlet to Shadow Lake we are on the John Muir Trail; then it branches off north to Thousand Island Lake. Our route continues up near Shadow Creek for about 3 km to Ediza Lake, where there are scattered campsites around the shores.

From here one can retrace one's steps to Agnew Meadows via Shadow Creek, but the experienced backpacker can make an interesting loop or shuttle to Devils Postpile. A faint trail switchbacks south from the southeast end of Ediza Lake up a steep, willow-covered slope. Parts of the trail are overgrown, and one should take care to stay to the left on the most heavily used trail to ensure arrival at Iceberg Lake.

At the top of the first rise, we see below the glacial cirque that holds Ediza Lake, and to the northwest, through a notch, there is a memorable view of Banner and Ritter. On the east, the massive black heights of Volcanic Ridge dominate the horizon. We ascend through several little alpine meadows covered with lupine, heather and pussypaws, and finally reach Iceberg Lake. From the outlet the footpath around the east side of the lake becomes lost occasionally in the talus as we ascend to the outlet of Cecile Lake. This stretch often has icy

Right: Iceberg Lake, Minarets

snow on it in early to mid season, and inexperienced backpackers *should be very cautious if attempting it.*

Cecile Lake has the choicest views of the Minarets, and one will certainly want a camera there. Our obscure, partly ducked route skirts the lake on its east side to the southeast end of the lake, from which we have awesome views of Clyde Minaret, Minaret Lake and Minaret Creek canyon. From here, one can either head back or drop down 500 feet to Minaret Lake, on the vague trail to the east.

A long return loop may be made from Minaret Lake to Agnew Meadows, or one may simply be met by car at Devils Postpile, or hitch-hike out from there. The Minaret Lake Trail (Backpack Trail #4) leads out to Devils Postpile. To make a complete loop back to Agnew Meadows, take the Minaret Lake Trail as far as Johnston Meadow and then head north on the Muir Trail to Shadow Lake. From there the first 5½ km of the Ediza Lake trail return one to Agnew Meadows.

BACKPACK TRAIL #8

Thousand Island Lake via the River Trail (12 km, 7½ mi.)

The River Trail, which parallels the upper Middle Fork of the San Joaquin River to its source, Thousand Island Lake, is the least scenic route to the lake. However, an interesting and dramatic loop returns from the lake via the High Trail (Backpack Trail #9).

Our route leaves the parking lot just north of Agnew Meadows Pack Station and follows the beginning of the Ediza Lake Trail (Backpack Trail #7) to a fork just beyond Olaine Lake. Here we take the right (N) fork and climb steeply up from the river for a while, until the trail's ascent becomes gentler under fairly dense lodgepole pines. The sound of the cascading San Joaquin River is a pleasant accompaniment to this dusty climb up the canyon. We cross several streamlets coming down from the Sierra crest on the east before arriving at the Agnew Pass Trail. (This lateral climbs steeply through open lodgepole pine and sagebrush to the High Trail, and then goes on to Agnew Pass.)

The River Trail continues up the canyon, passes the Garnet Lake lateral, and slants upward away from the river to join the High Trail coming in from the right (E). From this junction we climb ahead (N) toward Thousand Island Lake before leveling off in meadows containing several small tarns. Several trails branch off to numerous campsites her, but by keeping near the Middle Fork and heading toward Banner Peak, we reach Thousand Island Lake and a junction with the John Muir Trail (Backpack Trail # 1). Camping here is scenic, with magnificent views of the Ritter Range to the west. Sites near the outlet are exposed and windy but better sites may be found north and west of the lake where streamlets cascade down the slopes.

Red fox

BACKPACK TRAIL # 9

Thousand Island Lake via the High Trail (11 km, 7 mi.)

This alternative to taking the River Trail (Backpack Trail
8) to Thousand Island Lake affords panoramic views of the
Minarets, Mt. Ritter and Banner Peak, as well as glimpses down
into the deep, glaciated canyon of the Middle Fork San Joaquin
River. The High Trail can be combined with the River Trail to
form an exciting loop trip between Agnew Meadows and
Thousand Island Lake.

The High Trail begins at the parking lot north of Agnew
Meadows Pack Station. This trail starts with several long switchbacks in red-fir forest which take us up behind the pack station.
Then we emerge from timber into open sagebrush scrub and,
climbing steadily along the east wall of the Middle Fork canyon,
we come to a vista point opposite the U-shaped canyon of
Shadow Creek. This is one of the most impressive sights along
the route. The gouging power of glaciers during the Ice Ages is
attested to by the deeply scarred Middle Fork canyon and the
hanging valley of Shadow Creek—formed by a tributary glacier
—dropping steeply to the main valley below.

From this point the trail undulates along, trending upward,
through a ground cover of mostly sagebrush, bitterbrush, willow and some mountain alders. Each time the trail descends to
one of the many tributaries of the San Joaquin River, the
traveler will observe a lush growth of wildflowers, including
larkspur, lupine, shooting star, columbine, penstemon, monkey
flower, scarlet gilia and tiger lily.

Just before the High Trail begins its descent to meadowy
Badger Lakes, an unmarked cut-off to Agnew **Pass and Clark**

Lakes (Lateral Trail # 3) forks to the right (N). We continue toward Badger Lakes, crossing the Agnew Pass Trail, which connects Agnew Pass to the right (N) with the River Trail to the left (S) via a steep path. Just beyond Badger Lakes, the trail to Agnew Pass and Clark Lakes rejoins our route. Continuing on the High Trail, we roll gently through open lodgepole pine, and then switchback down to a junciton with the River Trail on the slopes above the upper reaches of the Middle Fork. From here we follow the River Trail for 1½ km to Thousand Island Lake, where the camping and views are as described in Backpack Trail # 8.

BACKPACK TRAIL # 10

Lake George Campground to Deer Lakes (9 km, 5½ mi.)

The Deer Lakes Trail along Mammoth Crest essentially dead-ends in a glaciated basin, the route down Deer Creek from the lakes being abandoned. This trail offers vistas of much of *Devils Postpile* quadrangle, rivaling those from Mammoth Mountain.

First we follow the Crystal Lake Trail (Day Hike # 2) until it branches left (S), then continue climbing in pumice to the right (W). Switchbacks take us up toward Mammoth Crest through lodgepole pine, silver pine and mountain hemlock into

a thinning stand of whitebark pine. Where the scattered trees
have been flattened into *krummholz* form by wind and snow,
granite-and-pumice footing gives way to reddish cinders.

Just below a fork in the trail we enter the 503,258-acre
John Muir Wilderness—California's largest—named for the
famed naturalist. This area, first set aside in 1931 (as the High
Sierra Primitive Area) by authority of the Secretary of Agriculture, extends from here southward along the Sierra crest to
the peaks south of Mt. Whitney. Inside this preserve we take
the right fork up to the prominent cinder cone in the west; on
our return we can come back by the left (S) fork, which crosses
a small crater. Much of the area of *Devils Postpile* quadrangle is
visible from the summit of this cone. We can make out both
the Middle Fork and the North Fork of the San Joaquin, the
Ritter Range, Mammoth Mountain, and Mammoth Crest. Mt.
Morrison and Bloody Mountain, in the *Mt. Morrison* quad, are
visible in the east.

Proceeding southeast across the west slope of the crest, the
trail crosses an arid-looking saddle with scattered whitebark
pines separated by large expanses of cindery, granity gravel.
Judging by the sparseness of vegetation and the exposure to
winds here, one may reasonably conclude that the precipitation
available to plants on this ridge might be no more than that which
defines an arid region: 10 inches or less annually. Since high winds
accompany most of the winter snowstorms that supply the bulk
of this region's moisture, and since winds are most intense on
summits like this, only a few inches of snow may accumulate
here, compared to the hundreds that build up on both sides of
the crest. So this saddle can possibly be considered arid, even
though it is in a region of moderately high precipitation.

Fish Valley comes into sight below as our route gets rocky and begins a steep ascent through a stand of whitebark pine. The path tops the ridge at 11,200 feet, and we can now see all the way to the White Mountains on the Nevada border to the east. In between lie Coldwater Canyon, Gold Mountain, and Glass Mountain ridge. (Here the trail goes off *Devils Postpile* quad to the east and enters *Mt. Morrison.*) From the ridge we round a shoulder and drop steeply down through whitebark pine to the outlet of the northernmost of the three Deer Lakes. Sheltered campsites are on the west and south sides. An inviting little beach beckons at the northwest corner of the lake.

Faint trails lead from this lake through meadows and dense but scrubby whitebark pine to the upper lake, where camping is most sheltered around the outlet. The cirque that these lakes lie in offers opportunities for leisurely wandering over talus slopes, moraines, and wet meadows thick with red and white heather, dwarf willow and Labrador tea. The lowest of the three lakes is the most heavily used, and it has the poorest campsites.

BACKPACK TRAIL # 11

Granite Creek Campground to Hemlock Crossing (14½ km, 9 mi.)

This trail is one of two in this guide which begin at a trailhead in the *Merced Peak* quadrangle, with road access from the west side of the Sierra. The other is the trail to 77 Corral. This route to Hemlock Crossing begins as the Isberg Trail at the northeast corner of Granite Creek Campground and proceeds up along the west bank of East Fork Granite Creek. Several signs indicate that this area is closed to motor vehicles.

The forest cover here consists mostly of large Jeffrey and lodgepole pines, with young white and red firs in the understory. When fires are absent, the shade-tolerant firs normally supplant the pines in forest succession. Otherwise, the fire-tolerant pines remain dominant. Wildflowers thriving along the sandy path include purplish lupine, white mariposa lily, and a prostrate member of the purslane family, pussy paws. Metal tags nailed to tree trunks 10-15 feet above the ground mark the way for snow surveyors who come in on skis during the winter to observe snow conditions. In mid season, especially during high winds or in a thunderstorm, pollen released by small male cones on the pines and firs gives everything a greenish cast.

Soon the trail comes out onto a brush-covered slope above East Fork Granite Creek and traverses through manzanita, huckleberry oak, buckbrush and gooseberry to Granite Creek Niche, where the East Fork rushes through a narrow gap—the "Niche"—between two granite shoulders. Camping is good here.

Leaving the Niche, we parallel the stream and soon arrive at a junction from where the Isberg Trail continues north to Yosemite National Park (as described in the High Sierra Hiking Guide to *Merced Peak*). Our route crosses East Fork Granite Creek, and then passes through a meadow that is being overrun by young lodgepole pines but is still open enough to have a cover of cottony knotweed, yellow meadow monkey flowers, lavender shooting stars and large-leaved corn lilies. We pass the Cora Creek Trail (Lateral Trail # 1) and the Stock Driveway to Soldier Meadow and then begin a long, rolling grind through lodgepole forest. Only the tinkling note of the dark-eyed junco and the errie fluting of the hermit thrush interrupt our solitude.

There are few hikers on this trail.

At each of several forks we keep left, and when we arrive at Chetwood Creek we have entered *Devils Postpile* quadrangle. At the next fork, we keep left, following blazes through lodgepole pine and red fir, and finally break out into open aspen and sagebrush. Our route then switchbacks up a dry slope, and we soon come to "Surprise Saddle." Here a fine vista of the west side of the Ritter Range sloping down into the North Fork of the San Joaquin River greets the eye. The classic U-shaped, glaciated canyons of Dike and Iron creeks, the knife-edged ridge of the Minarets, and extensive glacial polish offer a dramatic, first-hand view of the effects of glaciation. Off in the south, the confluence of the three forks of the San Joaquin River is evident, and down in the canyon below we can make out a snow-survey shelter on the North Fork.

Entering a mixed forest of red fir, mountain hemlock and silver pine, dotted with large fields of blue lupine, we begin a long descent to Hemlock Crossing. Our path leaves the *Devils Postpile* map briefly here and then re-enters it as we cross a small stream and start to drop in earnest toward the North Fork. The trail soon becomes extremely steep and rocky. Firs and hemlocks on this steep slope are permanently warped at their bases, due to the deep winter snows that bent them to the ground as seedlings and saplings. On this sharp drop down into the bottom of the canyon, patches of brush and mosquitoey swales dense with white-flowered Labrador tea and bracken alternate with stands of trees.

At the end of a 2000-foot descent, we intersect the Iron Creek Trail (a portion of Backpack Trail #3) near Hemlock Crossing. Camping is scenic here. The North Fork breaks

through the bedded rock strata it has been paralleling and
plunges into a large, cold pool, good for late-season swimming.
Views up and down the canyon are extraordinarily beautiful.
One can go on from here to the upper North Fork and Twin
Island Lakes, or loop back to Granite Creek Campground, using
the descriptions for Backpack trails # 3 and # 12 and Lateral
Trail # 1.

BACKPACK TRAIL # 12

Granite Creek Campground to 77 Corral (14½ km, 9 mi.)

Three miles of walking may be eliminated from this route if
the water in the forks of Granite Creek is low enough to allow
fording by motor vehicle. One may then drive east on Forest
Service Road 4S57 to summit 7527 feet, overlooking the North
Fork of the San Joaquin, and begin the hike there. However, in
early season—even later in years of high water—the hiker will
probably have to park in the campground and start out from
there.

From the campground at Granite Creek—which lies in the
Merced Peak quad—our route proceeds east up a Forest Service
road through insect-and disease-ridden lodgepole pines to
Soldier Meadow. Here two of the Forest Service's multiple-use
objectives can be observed. One is grazing. Cattle grazing in
forests is not incompatible with other uses if the carrying capa-
city of the land is not exceeded and the presence of the animals
is not detrimental to recreational, watershed, timber and wild-
life values. The other objective is watershed. In order to prevent
erosion and insure the quality of the water leaving this area, the
land behind the sign has been closed to all cross-country

motor-vehicle travel. Autos, trucks and bikes must stay on the
road, which is designated a "vehicle way" from here to the
North Fork overlook. (Timber sales are being planned in this
area, however, and conditions here may change greatly in the
next few years.)

We continue gently upward through transition forest, made
up of white and red fir, lodgepole and Jeffrey pine, and incense-
cedar. Pileated woodpeckers—crow-sized, brightly colored birds
that drill huge oval holes in insect-ridden trees—are not uncom-
mon here. Just before the end of the roadway, a sign says we
are on the Mammoth Trail System. One of the oldest trails
across the Sierra, it was used chiefly by stockmen, sheepherders
and prospectors going to Old Mammoth and the meadows in
between. In fact, sheep were taken across the North Fork for
summer grazing until 1963.

Before beginning our 1500-foot descent to Sheep Crossing,
we have excellent views in the east of the Ritter Range and the
North Fork canyon. The rocky trail passes through typical mid-
Sierra transition forest, including Jeffrey pine, sugar pine, white
fir, incense-cedar, and also the deciduous California black oak.
This vegetation is rather unusual for *Devils Postpile* quadrangle,
which is generally covered by forests of lodgepole pine, a
higher-elevation species than those encountered on this slope.

Numerous streamlets and springs occur along the trail and
give moisture to a variety of herbs, including orange Sierra lily,
red-and-yellow columbine, pink cranesbill, yellow groundsel
and lavender shooting star. Occasional azaleas covered with
fragrant white blooms perfume the air as we descend through
this delightfully varied forest. Near the bottom of the canyon,
large flocks of bandtailed pigeons can be seen in the California

black oaks, one of their favored foods being the acorns of the
trees.

At Sheep Crossing the trail crosses a suspension bridge over
North Fork San Joaquin River and immediately begins a series
of long switchbacks up the dry, west-facing wall of the canyon.
The contrast between the environment and the vegetation on
this side and those on the slope we just came down is an ecological lesson. Here the hot afternoon sun's rays strike the ground
almost perpendicularly. We see much more open ground, brush-
fields of manzanita and huckleberry oak, and a predominance
of black oak and Jeffrey pine—all characteristic of drier sites at
this elevation.

The ascent up this side of the canyon is much shorter than
the previous descent, and it is not too long before we are climbing only moderately into a cooler forest of fir, incense-cedar,
black oak and Jeffrey pine. At the upper end of Snake Meadow
a trail heads north to Earthquake Meadow, where it meets the
Iron Creek Trail (part of Backpack Trail #3) going to Iron
Creek and Hemlock Crossing. We continue eastward and upward toward 77 Corral, through cathedral-like stands of white
fir and Jeffrey pine. Mule deer, abundant here, are most likely
to be seen early or late in the day, when they feed most active-
ly. West Fork Cargyle Creek is a favored watering place, particularly in autumn, when water is scarce elsewhere. Scattered
clumps of bitter cherry delight the eye and the nose in early
season, when these short trees are in blossom, and they please
the eye again in fall, when their delicately yellow-tinted leaves
tremble in the breeze.

Beyond the creek our path crosses an opening richly endow-
ed in mid season with creamy Mariposa lilies, purple delphin-

iums and yellow monkey flowers, and then arrives at 77 Corral.
This place was named for 1877, a year of widespread drought
when this was one of the important green spots in the mountains for herders. Labeled *Corral Meadow* on the topo map, it
is little used today. Several campsites are located around the
meadow, but water may be a problem in late season. However,
routes to Twin Island Lakes and Devils Postpile (Backpack
Trail #3) and to Iron Lake pass through or start at 77 Corral,
so most hikers probably will use it only as a rest stop on their
way east or west across the mountains.

BACKPACK TRAIL #13

Glass Creek Meadow (7 km, 4½ mi.)

This unmarked and unmaintained trail begins in *Cowtrack
Mtn.* quadrangle and enters *Devils Postpile* in the northeast
corner after passing through a portion of *Mono Craters.* It
takes hikers to a little-travelled, but very lovely part of the quadrangle, that is, however, grazed by sheep under the Forest
Service's multiple-use management concepts.

We begin at the Division of Highways water intake on Glass
Creek about 1 km beyond Glass Creek Campground. Our route
follows the north side of Glass Creek under a cover of Jeffrey
pine and black cottonwood on a footing of pumice, obsidian
and granitic rocks. The clear, cold waters of Glass Creek bubble
alongside the trail. Staying high as the trail approaches Obsidian Dome and the pumice deepens, we come out onto a bench,
cross a road not shown on the topo, and continue on the again-
distinct trail beside the creek.

Our route then begins a steep ascent in pumice and dense willow thickets while the stream cascades cheerily to the south. After about 1 km the trail levels out in a stand of sagebrush with scattered lodgepole pine. The stream here is densely-covered by willows and promises good trout fishing for the careful angler.

After another short climb over heavily sheep-trailed pumice, we arrive at the east end of long (2½ km) Glass Creek Meadow. The Sierra crest at San Joaquin Mountain and Two Teats is visible ahead, and the backside of June Mountain lies to the north. The meadow itself is in a broad, U-shaped, glaciated valley with invading lodgepole pine forest on its margins.

Numerous streamlets flow into Glass Creek here and there are many possible campsites around the meadow with long vistas back toward Glass Mountain Ridge and the White Mountains near the Nevada border. If the sheep aren't around, you should be the only one here to enjoy the solitude of this place.

LATERAL TRAIL #1

The Niche to the North Fork Gaging Station (11 km, 7 mi.)

This lateral leads to good fishing and secluded camping on the San Joaquin River's North Fork. It leaves the Granite Creek Campground-Hemlock Crossing Trail (Backpack Trail #11) about 1 km north of the Niche, which lies just off the *Devils Postpile* quadrangle in *Merced Peak*.

Our dusty path first passes through a stand of red fir and lodgepole pine, and then, after crossing the Stock Driveway from Soldier Meadow, it begins dropping along the south side of Cora Creek (dry in late season). As the descent becomes steeper, the North Fork canyon and the west side of the Ritter Range near Iron Mountain come into sight. One cannot help noticing the contrast in vegetation between the cool, moist, north-facing slope we are walking down and the dry, south-facing slope across Cora Creek. Whereas this shadier side has a dense cover of white fir, willow and dwarf maple, the opposite side is mostly covered with brush, huckleberry oak and manzanita.

We continue to drop over several steplike benches down to North Fork San Joaquin, where there is a packer campsite. Fording is easy here only in late season, when snowmelt runoff is at a minimum; one must be cautious crossing the stream earlier in the year. Our route continues up the east side of the North Fork, where conditions are somewhat drier and the dominant plants are drought-resistant huckleberry oak, manzanita and juniper, with occasional Jeffrey pines.

Then the trail leaves the river and makes a short, steep ascent, up what becomes a cascading streamlet in early season, to the bench where Lily Lake lies behind a *roche moutonee* (see the chapter "Geology") above the river. This lake is undergoing succession from pond to forest, as litter and silt over the centuries have been filling it in and terrestrial plants have encroached from the surrounding forest. In late season red-brown bracken ferns, golden aspens and yellow willows give Lily Lake a welcome tint of fall color. Beyond Lily Lake we climb slightly and then descend to a good, well-developed campsite on a bench just above the river. About 400 meters beyond this campsite is a snow-survey shelter used by snow surveyors who come in on skis to measure the depth and density of winter snows.

These data are used to predict spring and summer runoff in the San Joaquin Valley.

A ducked trail ends about 400 meters beyond the shelter at a crossing to the gaging station on the west side of the river. Beyond the gaging station a faint, rough fishermen's trail continues upstream to the mouth of Iron Creek. A difficult, mostly cross-country route may be followed by the experienced hiker up the right side of the Iron Creek cataracts. Then, above the cataracts, a fording of Iron Creek may be made to the Iron Creek Trail (Backpack Trail # 3), where camping is good.

LATERAL TRAIL # 2
Beck Lakes Loop to Holcomb Lake and Ashley Lake
(2½ km, 1½ mi. to each)

This trail offers limited but secluded camping at the base of Iron Mountain and the southern extension of the Ritter Range.

The Holcomb Lake/Ashley Lake Trail takes off across King Creek from the Beck Lakes Loop (Main Trail # 5) about 400 meters south of Beck Cabin. Early in the season, the meadow at this junction is one of the best in the quadrangle for mosquitoes and therefore one of the worst for people; camping is poor at this time of the year.

We stay on the most-used trail, across exposed metamorphic and volcanic rocks dotted with mountain hemlock and lodgepole pine. Ahead, Iron Mountain looms tall and dark. After ¾ km of easy walking we come to the signed junction of the routes to Holcomb Lake and Ashley Lake. Our route to Holcomb Lake goes right, and we head up a gully with low walls of metamorphic rock on both sides. The path soon emerges from this gully and drops around the northeast corner of small, warm Noname Lake. Camping here is fair. Beyond this lake we pass a small pond and then arrive at Holcomb Lake. Fair campsites are scattered around the lake. During early and mid season, willow thickets around the lake offer nesting and feeding cover and song perches for the natty, distinctively marked white-crowned sparrow, a summer resident in much of the High Sierra that adds much to one's wilderness experience.

Back at the trail junction, Ashley Lake lies to the left. Bound for it, we cross the Holcomb Lake outlet stream, and the trail soon disapears, near a big bend in the creek from Ashley Lake. However, a short cross-country ramble up either side of the Ashley Lake outlet (stay near the stream!) under mountain·hemlock and whitebark pine brings one to the lake. Campsites are scarce, but Iron Mountain and its glacier looming above make this a much more scenic spot than Holcomb Lake. Iron Mountain is easily climbed from Ashley Lake (see *A Mountaineer's Guide to the High Sierra*).

LATERAL TRAIL # 3

High Trail to Agnew Pass, Clark Lakes and Badger Lakes

(3 km, 2 mi.)

This lateral from the High Trail (Backpack Trail # 9) takes us over the Sierra crest at Agnew Pass into the drainage of Rush Creek at Clark Lakes. (For trail connections beyond Clark Lakes, this lateral returns to the High Trail just west of Badger Lakes.

About 1½ km southeast of Badger Lakes, the High Trail from Agnew Meadows begins a gentle descent. Here our signed lateral to Agnew Pass and Clark Lakes forks to the right (N). We take it and traverse a slope covered with sagebrush and scattered lodgepole pines. Purplish mountain aster, scarlet gilia and yellowish mule ears are seen on this slope from mid to late season. Before arriving at Agnew Pass, we pass an unmarked trail to the right (E) which goes toward the saddle between Carson Peak and San Joaquin Mountain. However, it is no longer maintained and is very difficult to follow. Beyond this junction our route soon intersects the Agnew Pass Trail, and we turn right (N) onto it. A few meters up this trail we cross Agnew Pass at Summit Lake, where camping is good from early to mid season. Later, the water becomes stagnant.

About 400 meters beyond Agnew Pass our trail circles the largest of the Clark Lakes, and we pass the trail to Lower Rush Meadow and Gem Lake (described in the High Sierra Hiking Guide to *Mono Craters*) at its outlet. Camping is good east and west of the lake near the open meadowy areas.

The trail continues around the west side of this lake and climbs through open whitebark pine and mountain hemlock past several other lakes of the Clark Lakes group, which may be dry in late season after a mild winter. Beyond the last of the Clark Lakes, we glimpse Thousand Island Lake and Banner Peak in the west before dropping through open lodgepole, sagebrush and snowberry toward Badger Lakes, visible below. Our route rejoins the High Trail about 400 meters west of Badger Lakes.

Right: the largest Clark Lake

LATERAL TRAIL # 4

Lower Marie Lake (3 km, 2 mi.)

Lower and Upper Marie Lakes are high-elevation glacial lakes which offer exhilarating and secluded camping close to the heavily travelled John Muir Trail.

The newly constructed trail to Marie Lakes takes off from the Muir Trail northbound (Backpack Trail # 1) about 1 km north of Rush Creek. It switchbacks gently upward on granite and then levels off some through meadows with scattered patches of willows and whitebark pines. Numerous campsites with excellent views present themselves down toward the Marie Lakes outlet stream below.

Our well-graded route soon resumes its switchbacking ascent, now up the south wall of the canyon, where lupine plus alpine sorrel and other high-elevation flowers can be seen from mid to late season. In early season here the trail is likely to be covered with late-lingering snow, so watch for the ducks marking the route.

We next surmount a ridge with superb views of the Ritter and Cathedral ranges close at hand to the west, as well as the more distant peaks of the Sierra crest to the east. After a short descent, we arrive at the northeast corner of Lower Marie Lake where scattered camps can be made in the rocks near the outlet. Camping here is exposed and windy but highly scenic, with Mt. Lyell and Rodger Peak looming above to the west. A short cross-country jaunt along the west side of the lake takes one to Upper Marie Lake, 1½ km away.

Books

Farquhar, Francis P., *History of the Sierra Nevada*. Berkeley: U.C. Press, 1969

Hill, Mary, *Geology of the Sierra Nevada*. Berkeley: U.C. Press, 1975

McMinn, Howard E. and Evelyn Maino, *Pacific Coast Trees*. Berkeley: U.C. Press, 1959

Manning, Harvey, ed., *Mountaineering, the Freedom of the Hills*. Seattle: The Mountaineers, 1974

Munz, Philip A., *California Mountain Wildflowers*. Berkeley: U.C. Press, 1969

Peterson, P. Victor and P. Victor, Jr., *Native Trees of the Sierra Nevada*. Berkeley: U.C. Press, 1975

Peterson, Roger Tory, *A Field Guide to Western Birds*. Boston: Houghton, 1968

Robbins, Chandler, S., *et al.*, *Birds of North America*. New York: Golden, 1966

Sheridan, Michael F., *Guidebook to the Quaternary Geology of the East-Central Sierra Nevada*. Phoenix: 1971

Starr, Walter A. Jr., *Starr's Guide to the John Muir Trail*. San Francisco: Sierra Club, 1970

Storer, Tracy I. and Robert L. Usinger, *Sierra Nevada Natural History*. Berkeley: U.C. Press, 1963

Voge, Hervey and Andrew J. Smatko, *Mountaineers Guide to the High Sierra*. San Francisco: Sierra Club, 1972

Pamphlets

Huber, N. K., and Rinehart, C. D., *Cenozoic Volcanic Rocks of the Devils Postpile Quadrangle, Eastern Sierra Nevada, California*. U.S. Geological Survey, 1967

U.S. Department of Agriculture, Forest Service, *Search for Solitude*. Washington, 1970

Other Wilderness Press Publications

Sierra North (Third edition, 1976)

The Pacific Crest Trail, Vol. 1 (revised 1975)

High Sierra Hiking Guide to *Merced Peak* (1973)

High Sierra Hiking Guide to *Mono Craters* (1975)

High Sierra Hiking Guide to *Mt. Abbot* (revised 1973)

Index

Agnew Meadows 24, 62, 66, 68
Agnew Pass 67, 68, 69, 81, 82
Anona Lake 55
Ashley Lake 80, 81
aspen 13

Badger Lakes 68, 69, 81, 82
Banner Peak 1, 62
Barrett, Lake 25, 26
Beck Cabin 55, 56
Beck Lakes 35, 55, 56, 80
Bench Canyon 51
Boundary Creek 31, 33

Cargyle Creek 47
Cargyle Creek, East Fork 47
Cargyle Creek, West Fork 76
Cargyle Meadow 47
Cascade Valley 57, 61
Catherine, Lake 51
Cecile Lake 64, 66
Chetwood Creek 73
Clark Lakes 68, 69, 81, 82
Cold Creek 58
Cora Creek 79
Corral Meadow 47, 77
Crater Creek 33, 58
Crater Meadow 33, 41, 42
Crater Meadow, Upper 33, 42
creeper, brown 18
Crystal Lake 28

Deer Creek 42
Deer Lakes 69, 71
Devils Postpile 2, 5, 40, 44, 66
Devils Postpile National Monument
   1, 4, 24, 35, 40, 44, 52, 55, 57
Dike Creek 49
Donohue Pass 35, 39
Duck Creek 42, 43, 61
Duck Lake 43

Earthquake Meadow 48
Ediza Lake 62, 64
Emerald Lake 37
Fern Lake 55
finch, gray-crowned rosy 17
fir, red 11
fir, white 12
Fish Creek 21, 57, 59, 61
Fish Valley 58, 59

Garnet Lake 21, 37, 67
George, Lake 24, 25, 26, 28, 69
Glacier Pass 52
glaciers 6
Gladys Lake 36
Glass Creek 24, 77, 78
Glass Creek Meadow 77, 78
Gold Rush 3
Granite Creek 71, 74
Granite Creek, East Fork 71, 72
Granite Creek Campground 24

Headquarters Meadow 47
hemlock, mountain 12
Hemlock Crossing 49, 71, 73
Holcomb Lake 56, 80, 81
Horseshoe Lake 24, 32, 34

Iceberg Lake 64
Indians, Paiute 3
Indians, Yokut 3
Iron Creek 48, 80
Island Crossing 59
Island Pass 39

John Muir Trail 21, 33, 34, 35,
   36, 39, 40, 42, 43, 44, 52, 57,
   64, 66, 67
John Muir Wilderness 4, 28, 33,
   70
Johnston Meadow 66
junco, dark-eyed 16

King Creek 45, 55

Lily Lake 79
Long Canyon 61

Mammoth City 4
Mammoth Mountain 1, 5, 29
Mammoth Pass 4, 5, 29, 30, 34
Marie Lakes 39, 84
McGee Pass 44
McLeod Lake 32, 34
Minaret Creek 35, 36, 53
Minaret Lake 35, 52, 53, 66
Minaret Summit 1, 2
Minarets 1, 53, 62, 66
Minarets Wilderness 4, 49, 57
Minnow Creek 61

Noname Lake 81
nutcracker, Clark 14

Olaine Lake 62, 66
ouzel 16

pine, Jeffrey 8
pine, lodgepole 7
pine, silver 9
pine, whitebark 10
pioneer species 7
pumice 5
Purple Creek 61
Purple Lake 21, 43

Rainbow Falls 31, 40, 57
Red Cones 33, 41
Reds Meadow 4, 24, 31, 32, 33,
    34, 40, 57
Ritter, Mt. 1, 62
robin 14
roche moutonee 6
Rosalie Lake 36
Rush Creek 39

San Joaquin River, Middle Fork
    1, 5, 6, 31, 35, 37, 40, 44, 62,
    66, 68
San Joaquin River, North Fork
    48, 51, 73, 74, 76, 78, 79
Second Crossing 59
77 Corral 47, 71, 74, 77
Shadow Creek 6, 36, 37, 64
Shadow Lake 21, 35, 36, 62, 64,
    66
Sharktooth Creek 59
Sheep Crossing 76
Slide Creek 50
Smith, Jedediah 3
Snake Meadow 76
snow plant 45
Soda Spring Meadow 35
Soldier Meadow 74
Stairway Creek 46
Stairway Meadow, Lower 46
Starr, Jr., Walter A. 31
Stevenson Meadow 50
Summit Lake 82
Summit Meadow 4, 45, 46, 55
Superior Lake 56

T. J. Lake 25, 26
Third Crossing 61
Thousand Island Lake 1, 21, 37,
    66, 67, 68, 69
thrush, hermit 15
Trinity Lakes 36
Tully Hole 40, 44
Twin Island Lakes 44, 52, 74
Twin Lakes 24, 29

Virginia, Lake 43
Vivian Lake 36

Walker, Joseph 3